AUGUST 50 COLORING PAGES FOR OLDER KIDS RELAXATION

SHIH CHIEN HUA

PUBLISHED BY:
SHIH CHIEN HUA
Copyright © 2018

SEABIRD SHOP >50FOR

FB FAN PAGE

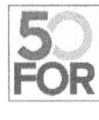

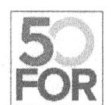

Disclaimer
The information contained in this book is for general information purposes only. The information is provided by the authors and while we endeavor to keep the information up to date and correct, we make no representations or warranties of any kind, express or implied, about the completeness, accuracy, reliability, suitability or availability with respect to the book or the information, products, services, or related graphics contained in the book for any purpose. Any reliance you place on such information is therefore strictly at your own risk.

AUGUST 1ST

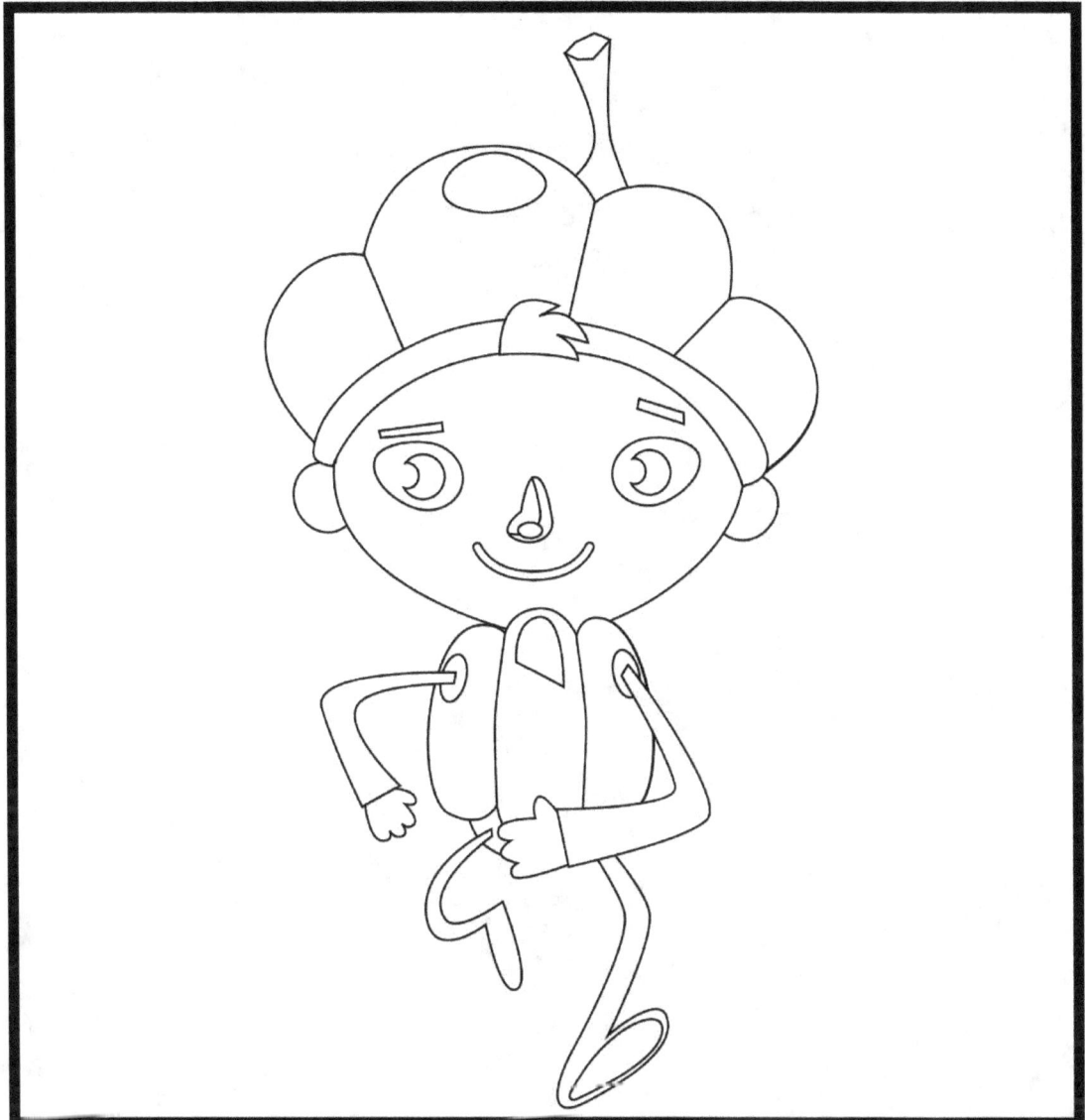

note:

_____

_____

_____

AUGUST 2ND

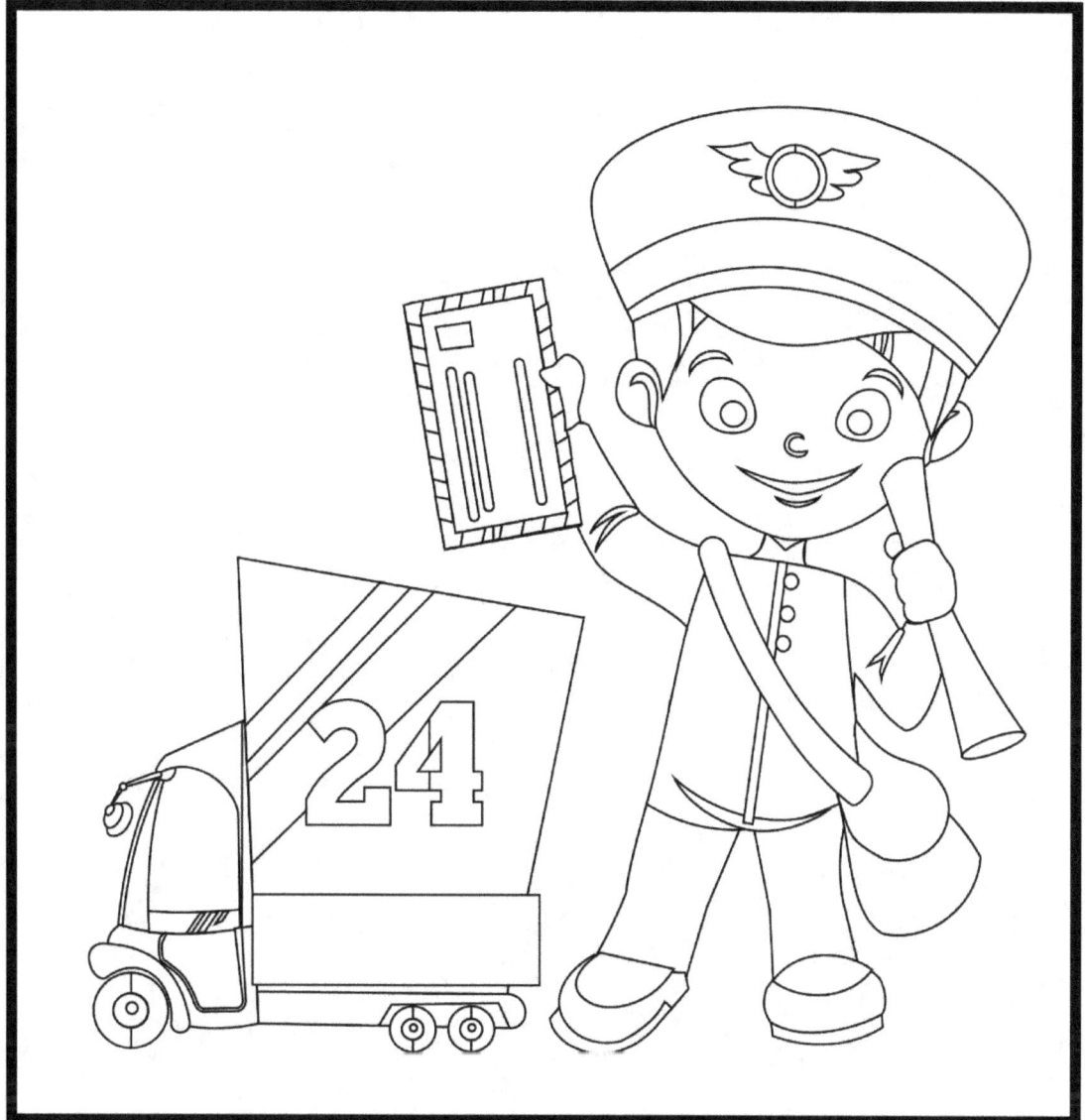

note:

_____

_____

_____

AUGUST 3RD

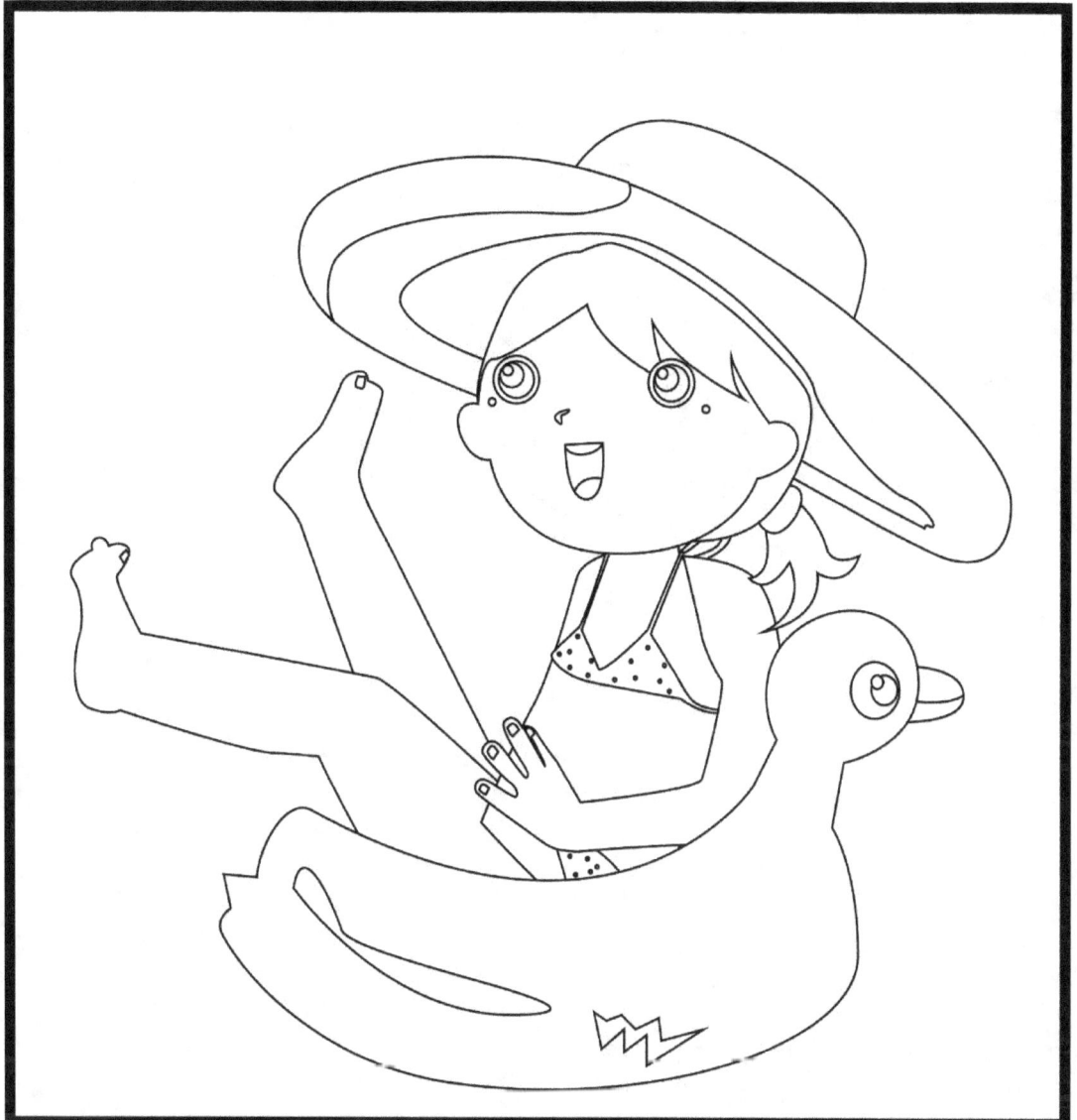

note:

_____

_____

_____

AUGUST 4TH

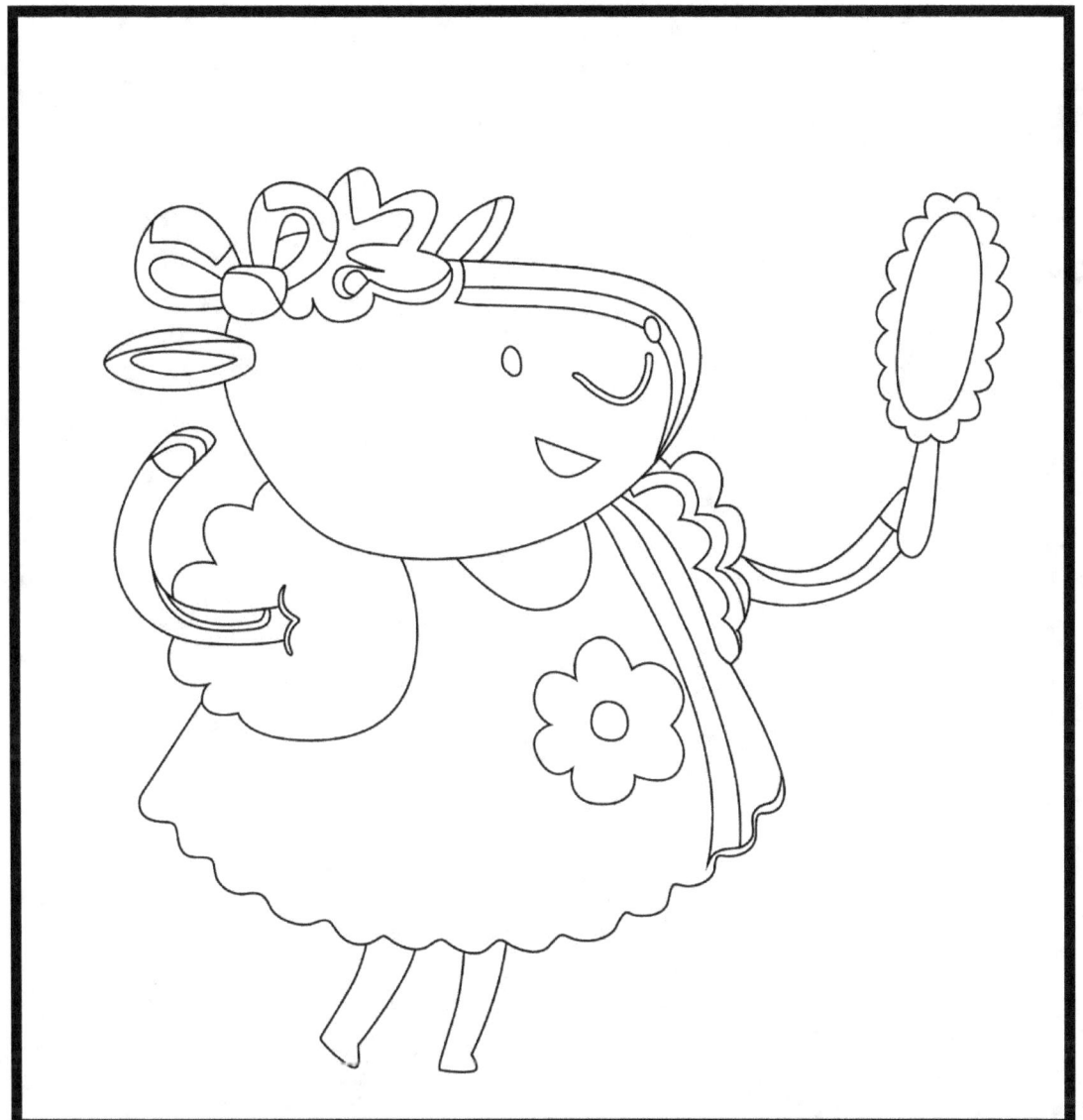

note:

_____

_____

_____

AUGUST 5TH

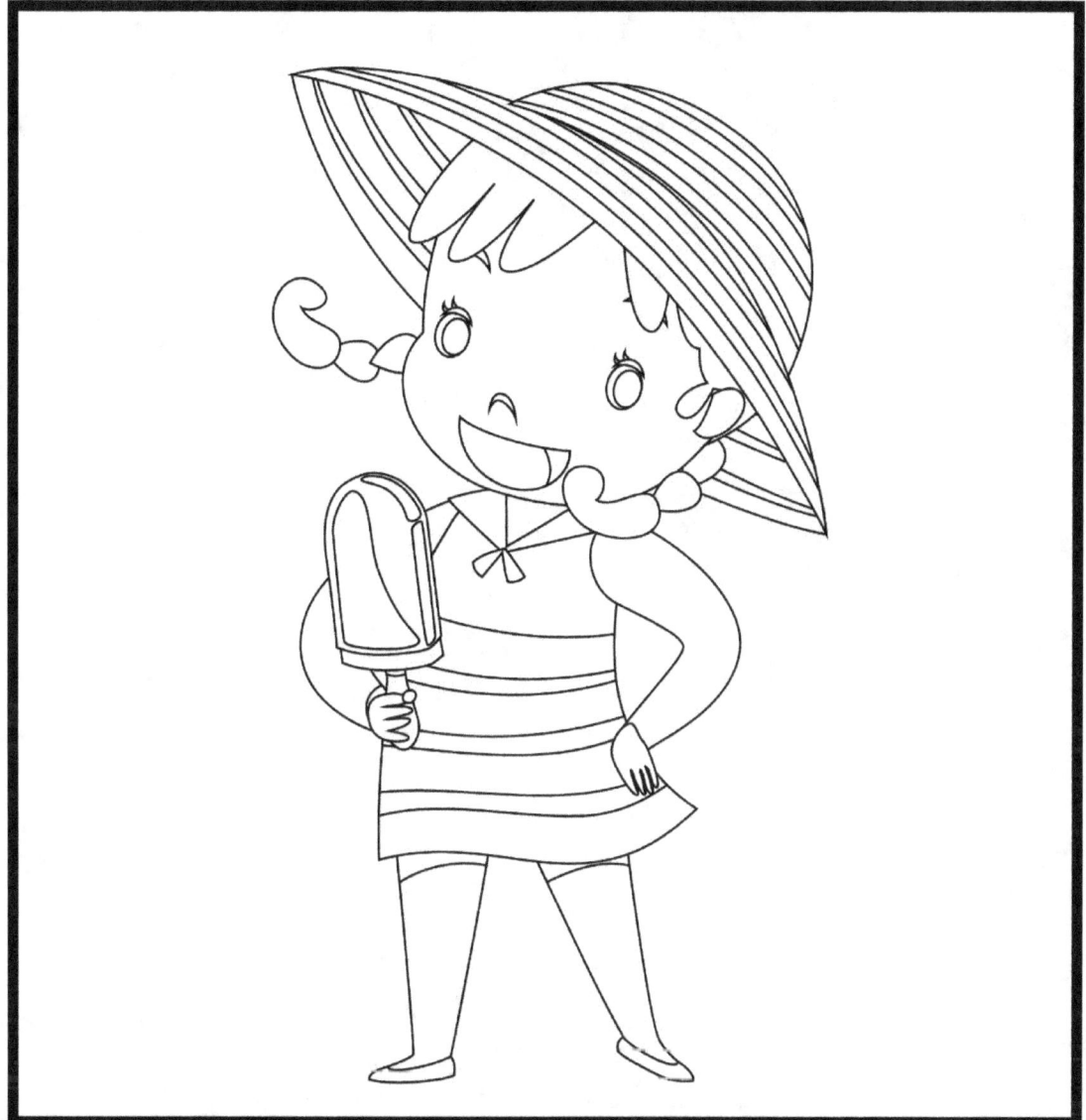

note:
_____

_____

_____

AUGUST 6TH

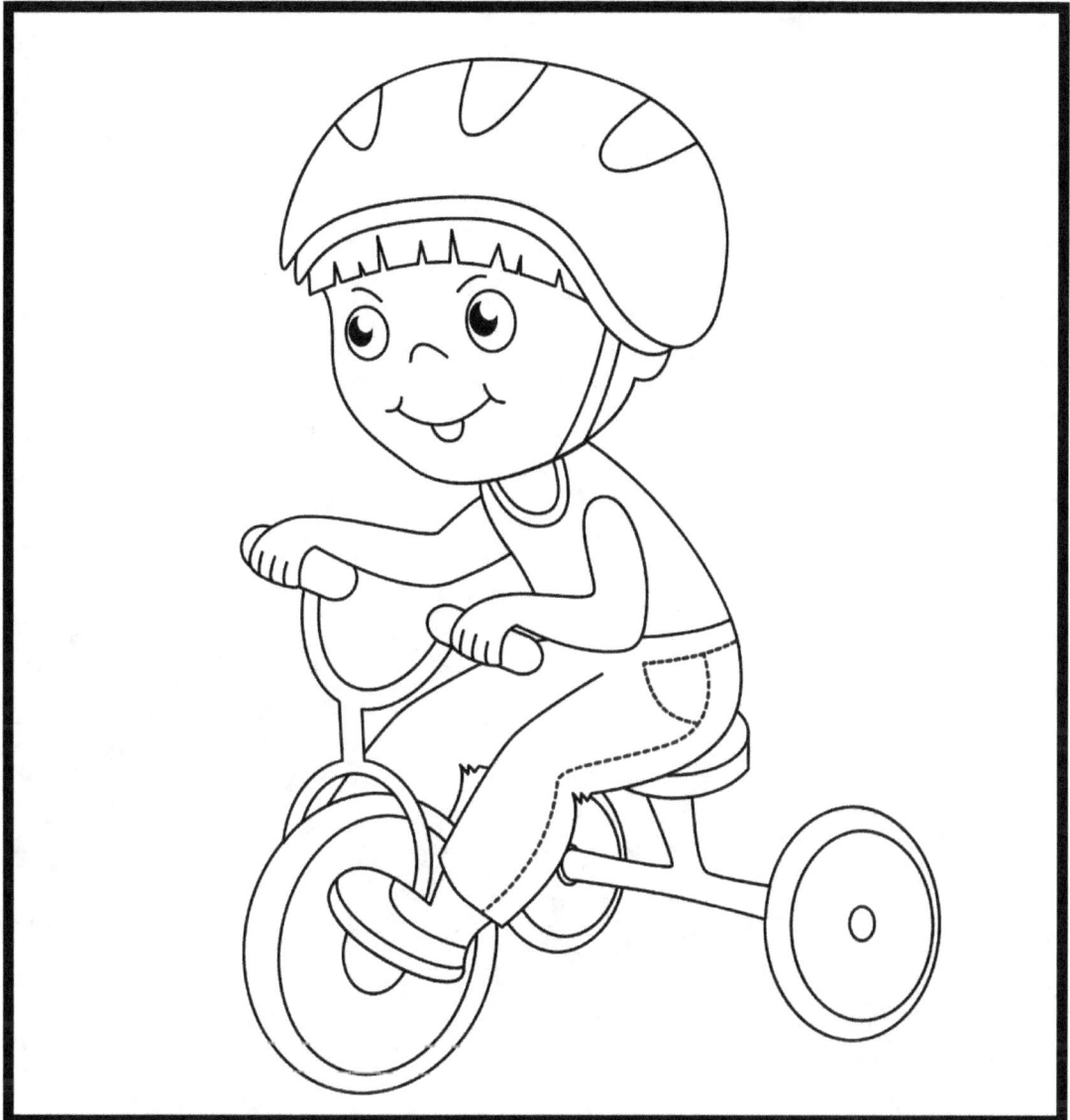

note:

_____

_____

_____

AUGUST 7TH

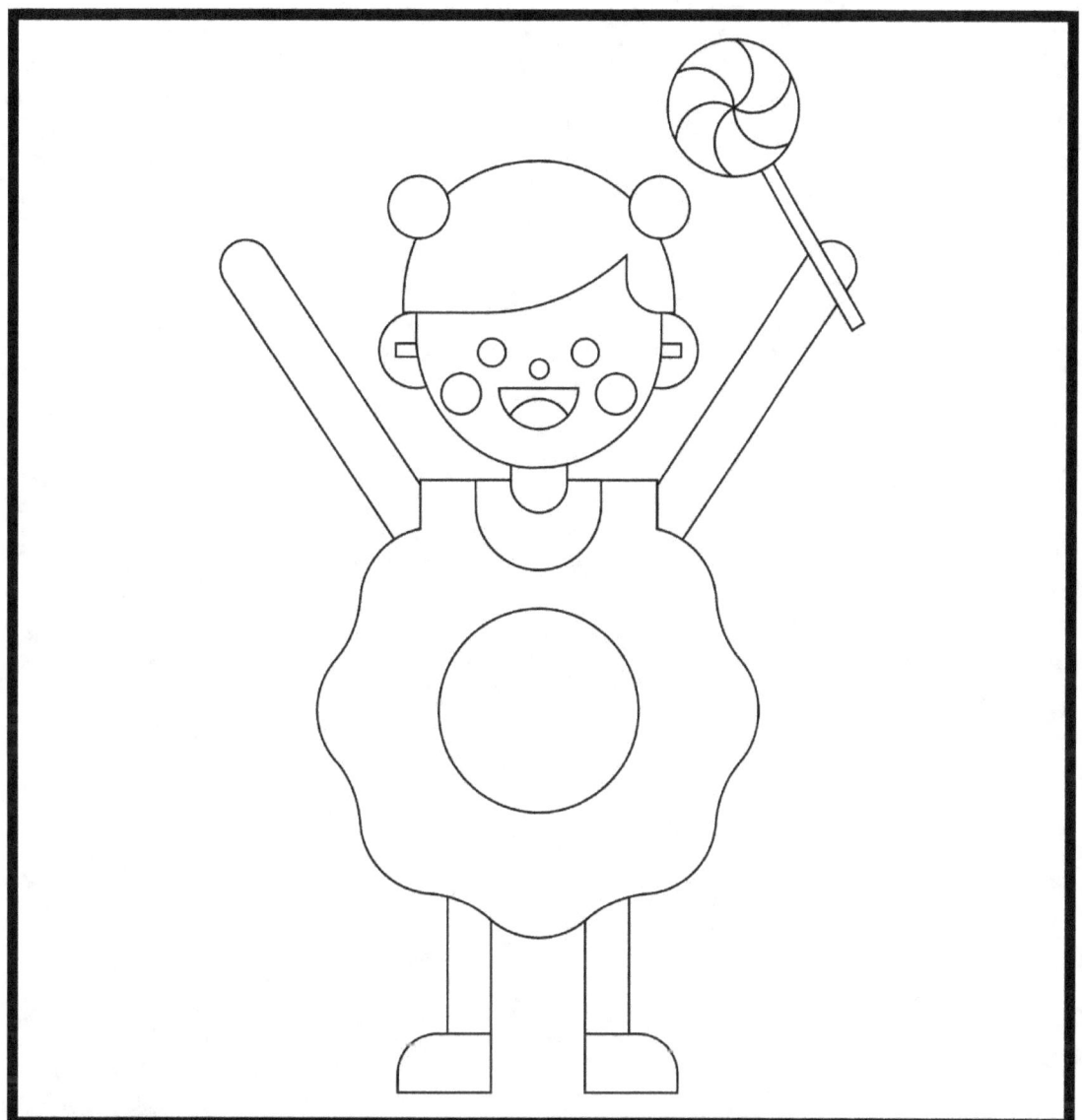

note:

_____

_____

_____

AUGUST 8TH

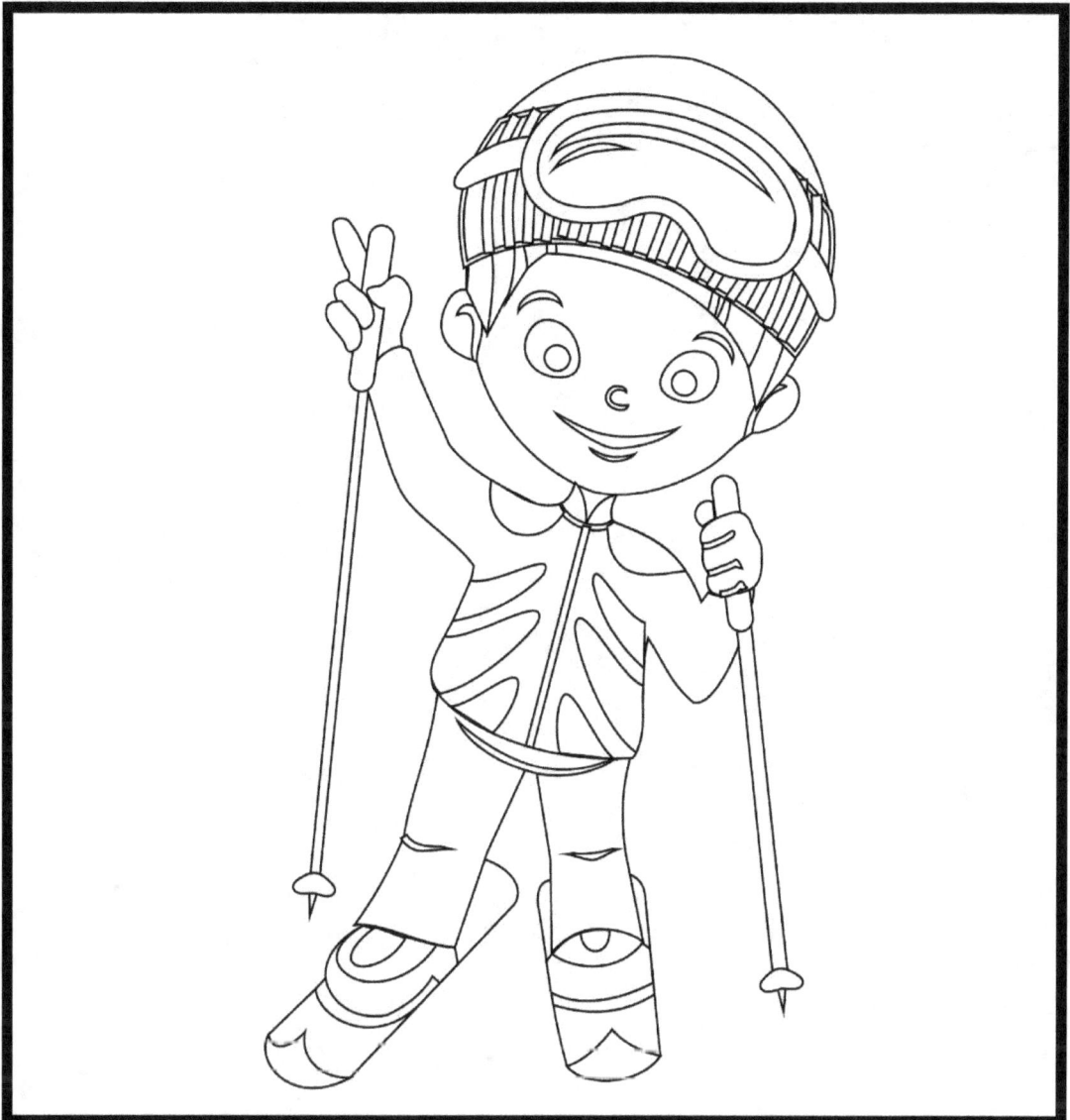

note:

_____

_____

_____

AUGUST 9TH

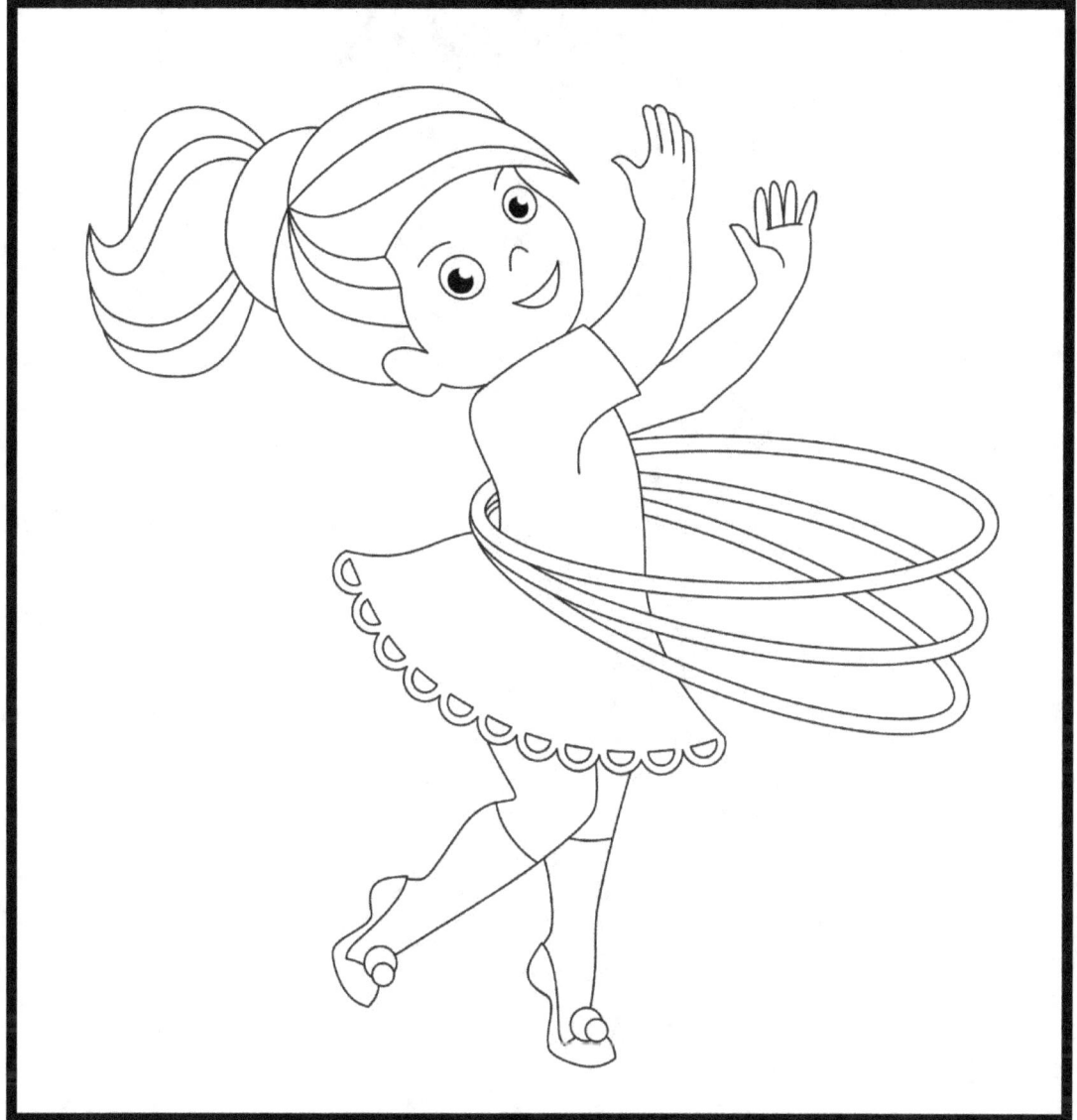

note:

_____

_____

_____

AUGUST 10TH

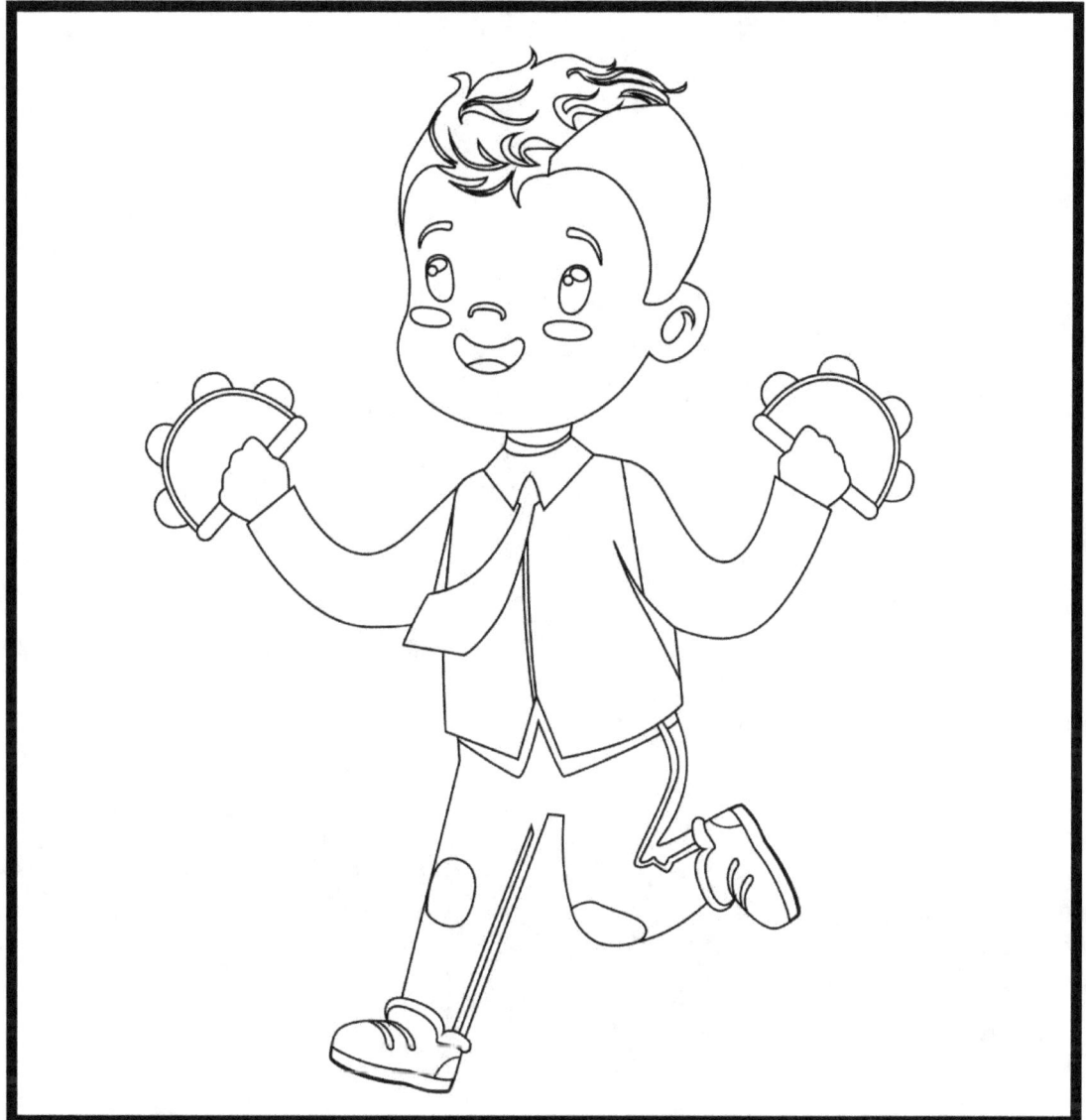

note:
_____
_____
_____

AUGUST 11TH

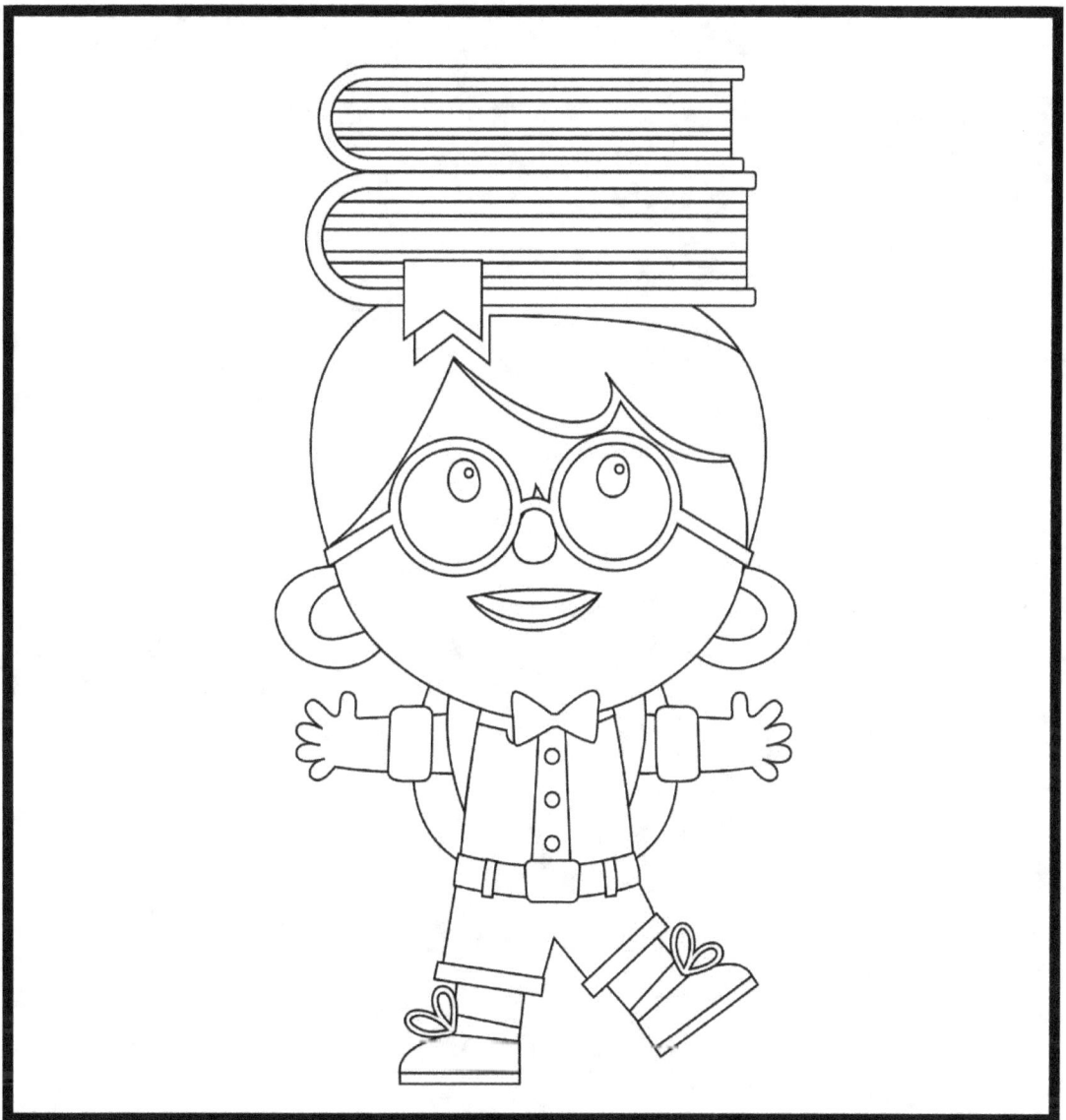

note:

_____

_____

_____

AUGUST 12TH

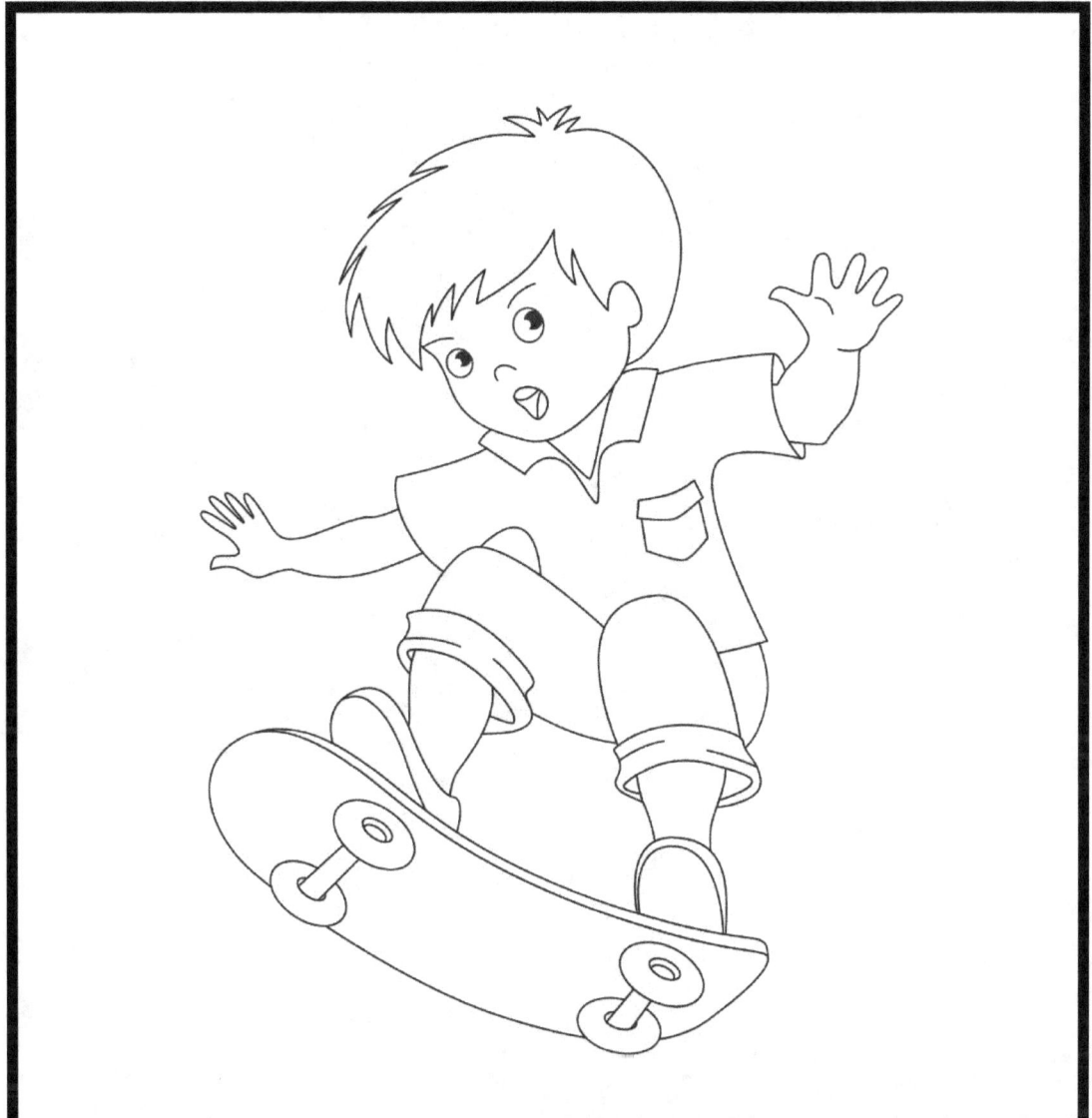

note:

_____

_____

_____

AUGUST 13TH

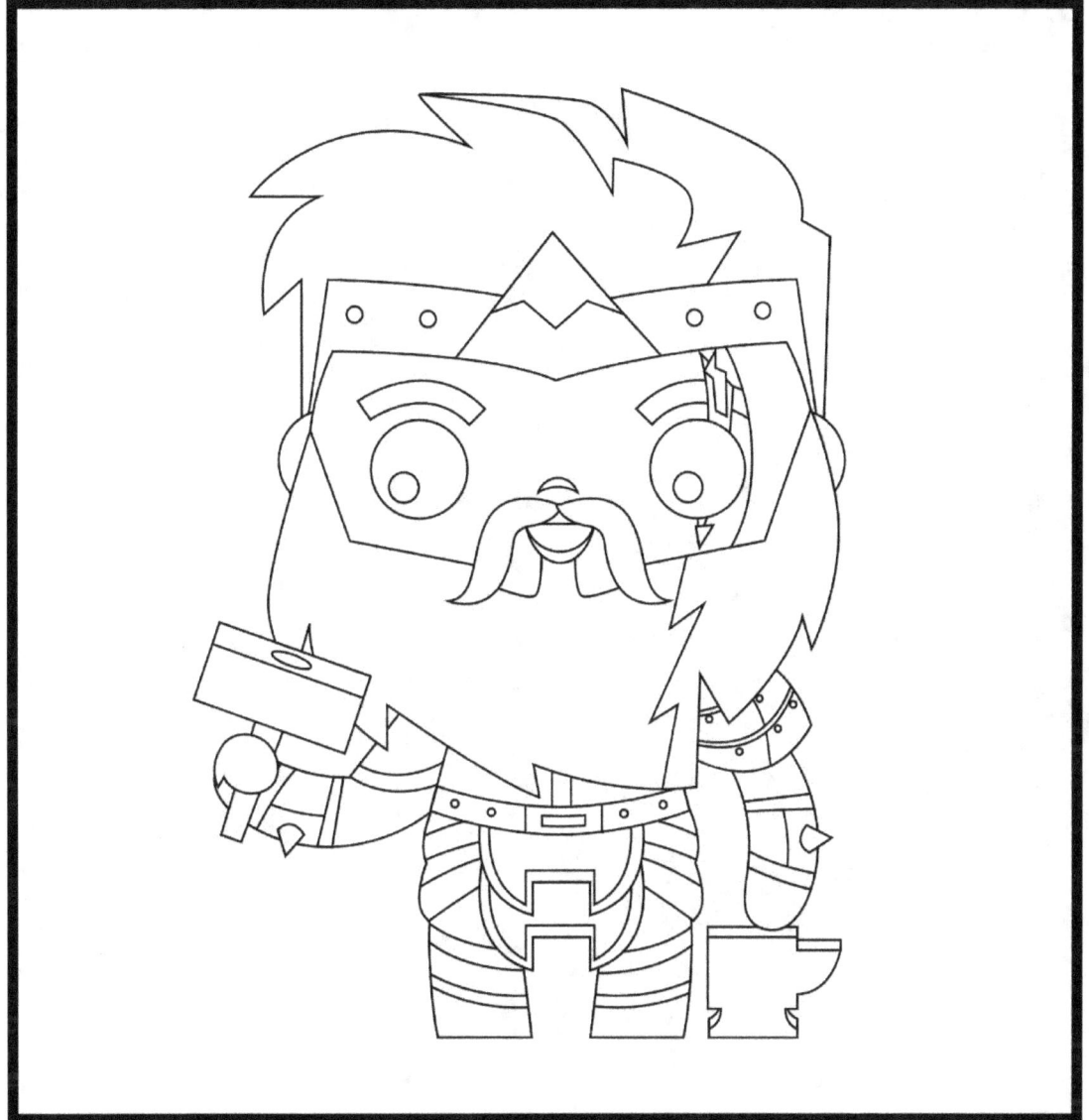

note:

_____

_____

_____

AUGUST 14TH

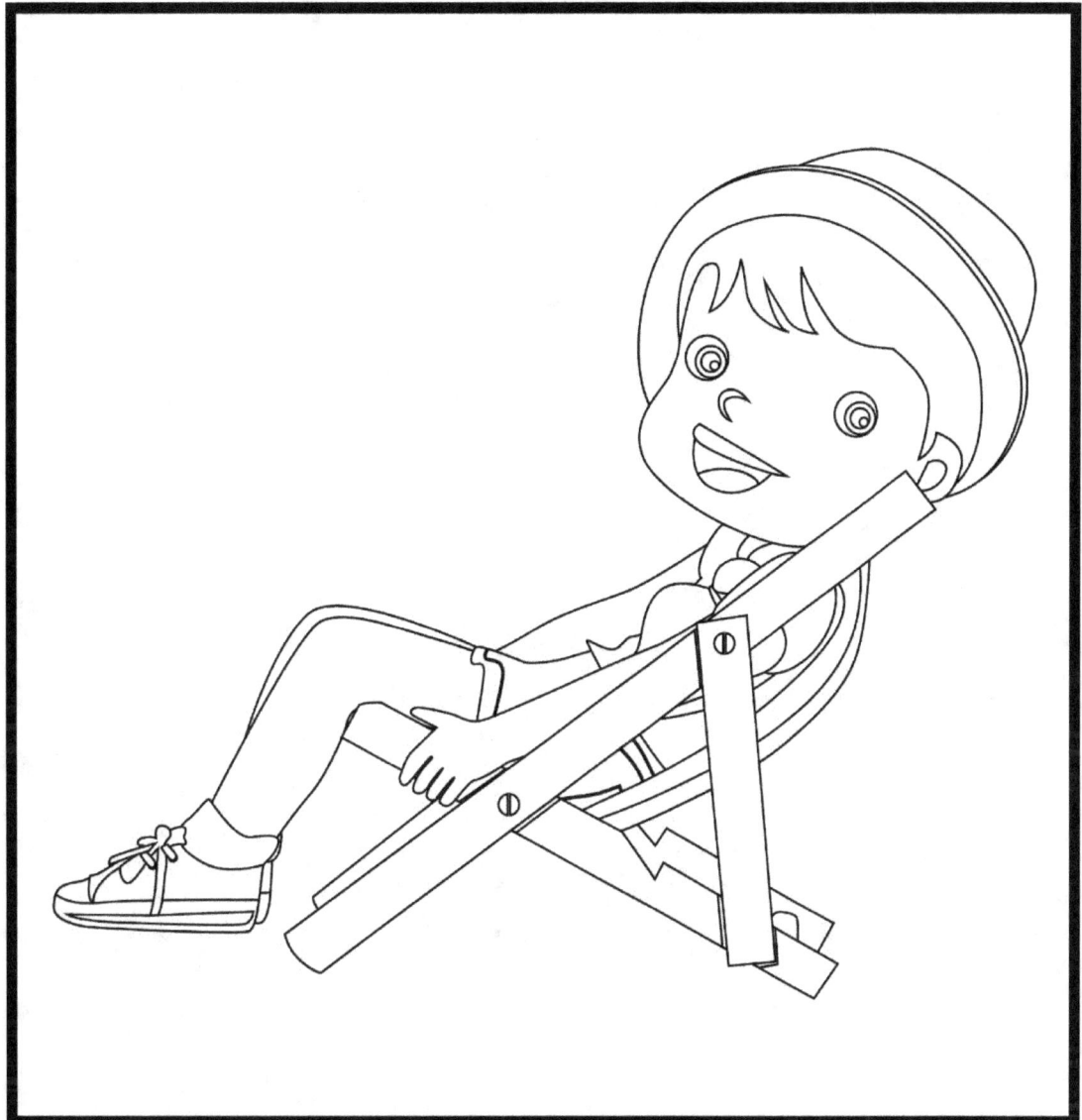

note:

_____

_____

_____

AUGUST 15TH

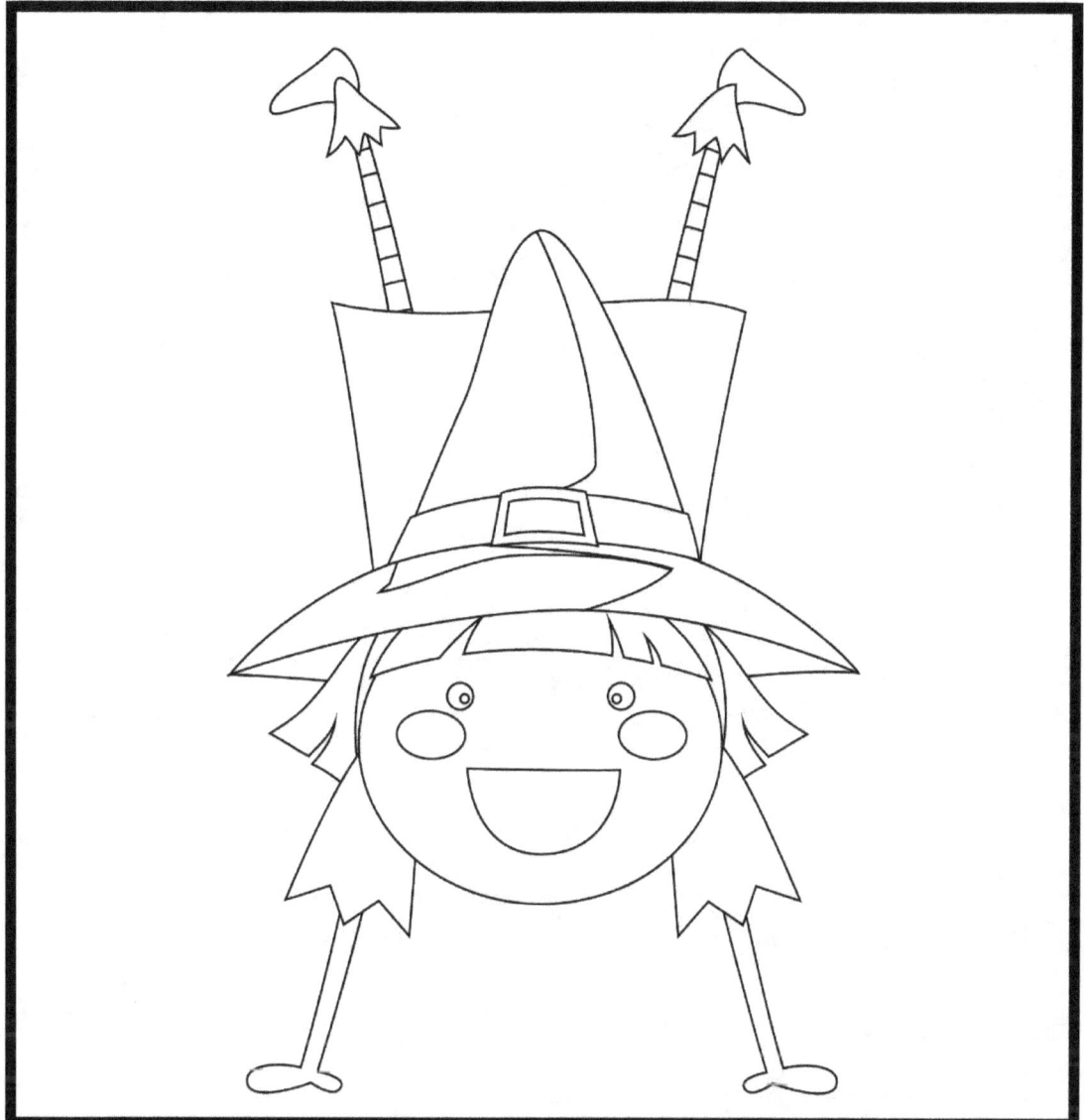

note:

_____

_____

_____

AUGUST 16TH

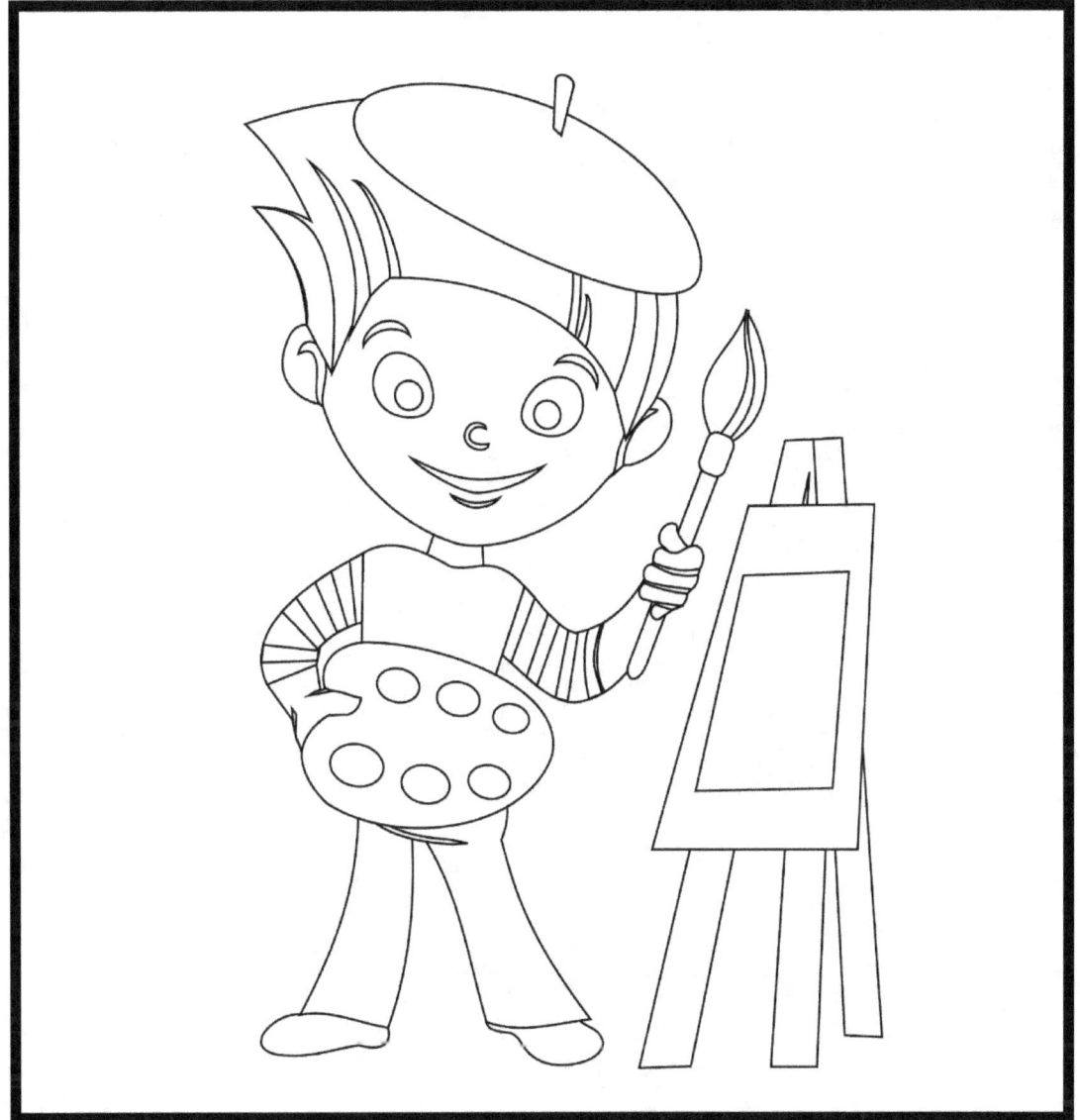

note:

_____

_____

_____

AUGUST 17TH

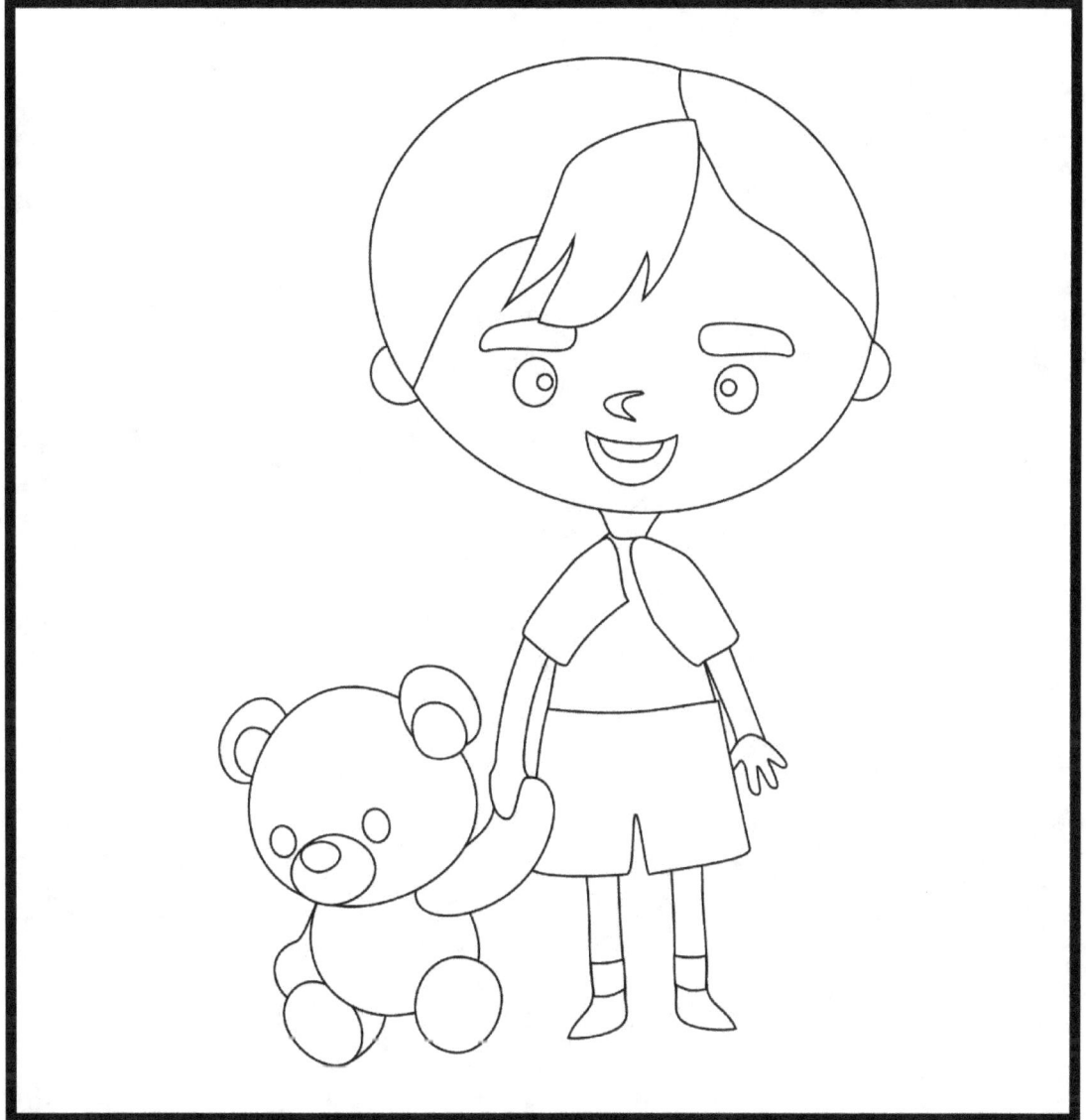

note:

_____

_____

_____

AUGUST 18TH

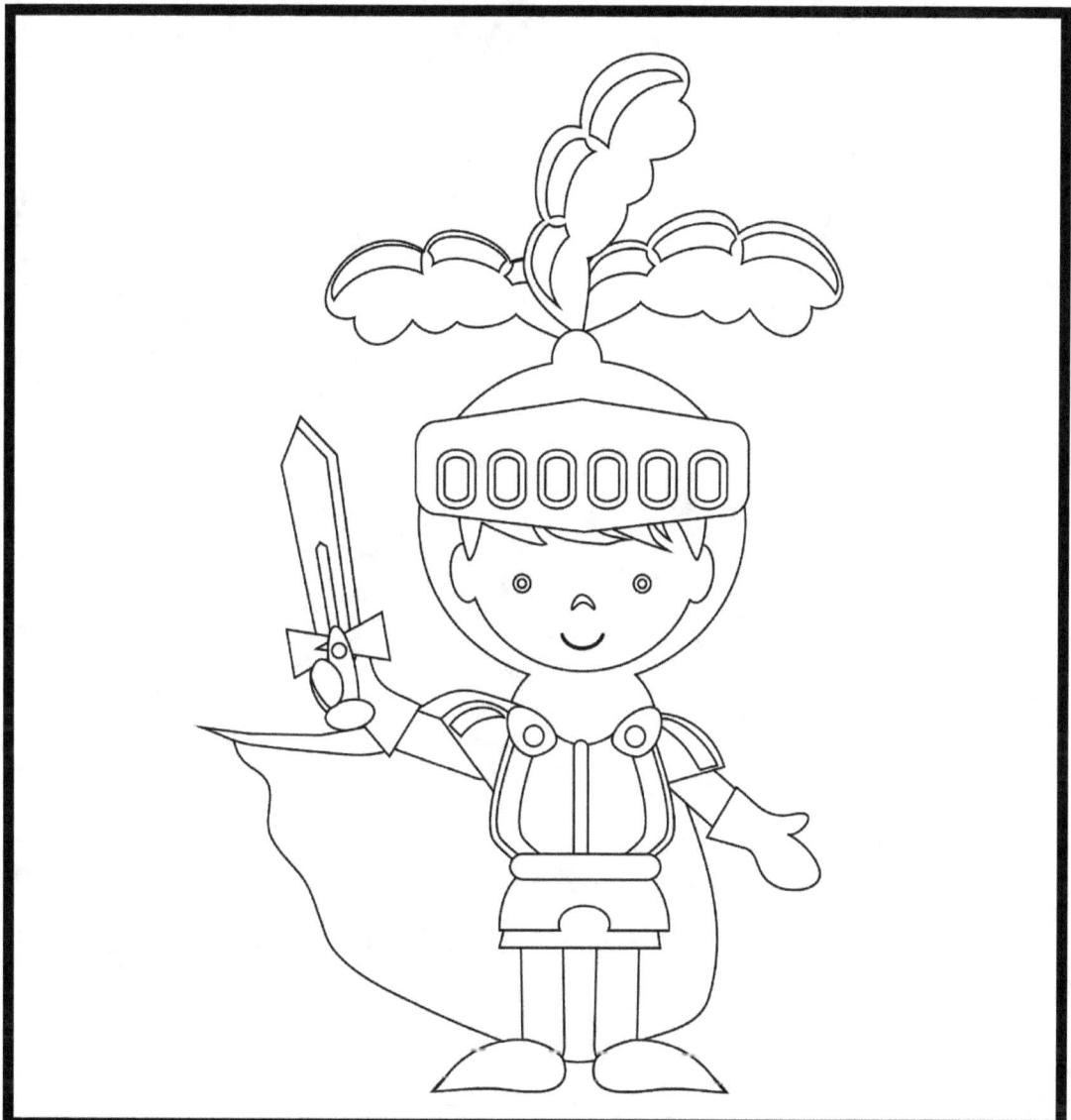

note:

_____

_____

_____

AUGUST 19TH

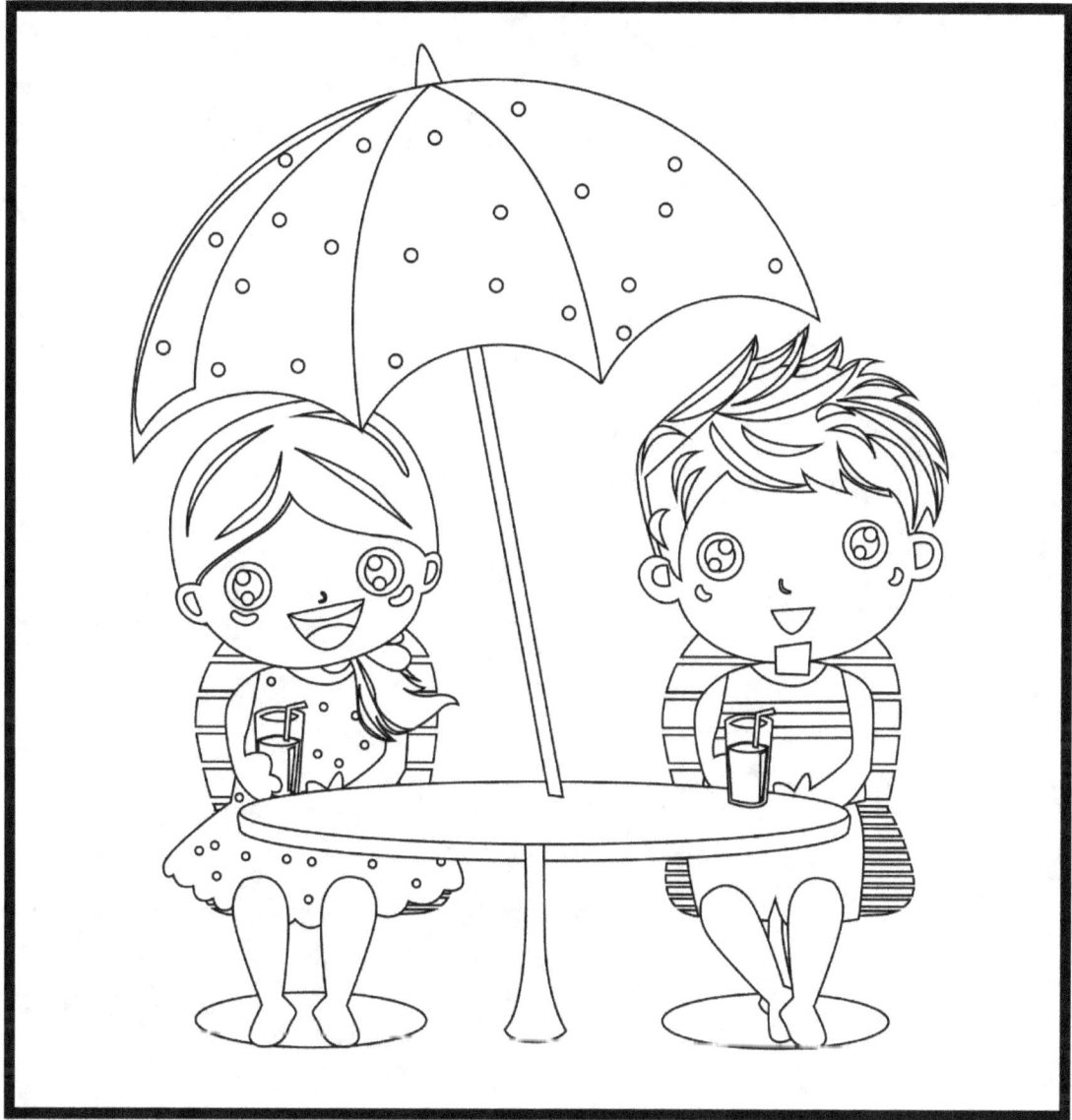

note:

_____

_____

_____

AUGUST 20TH

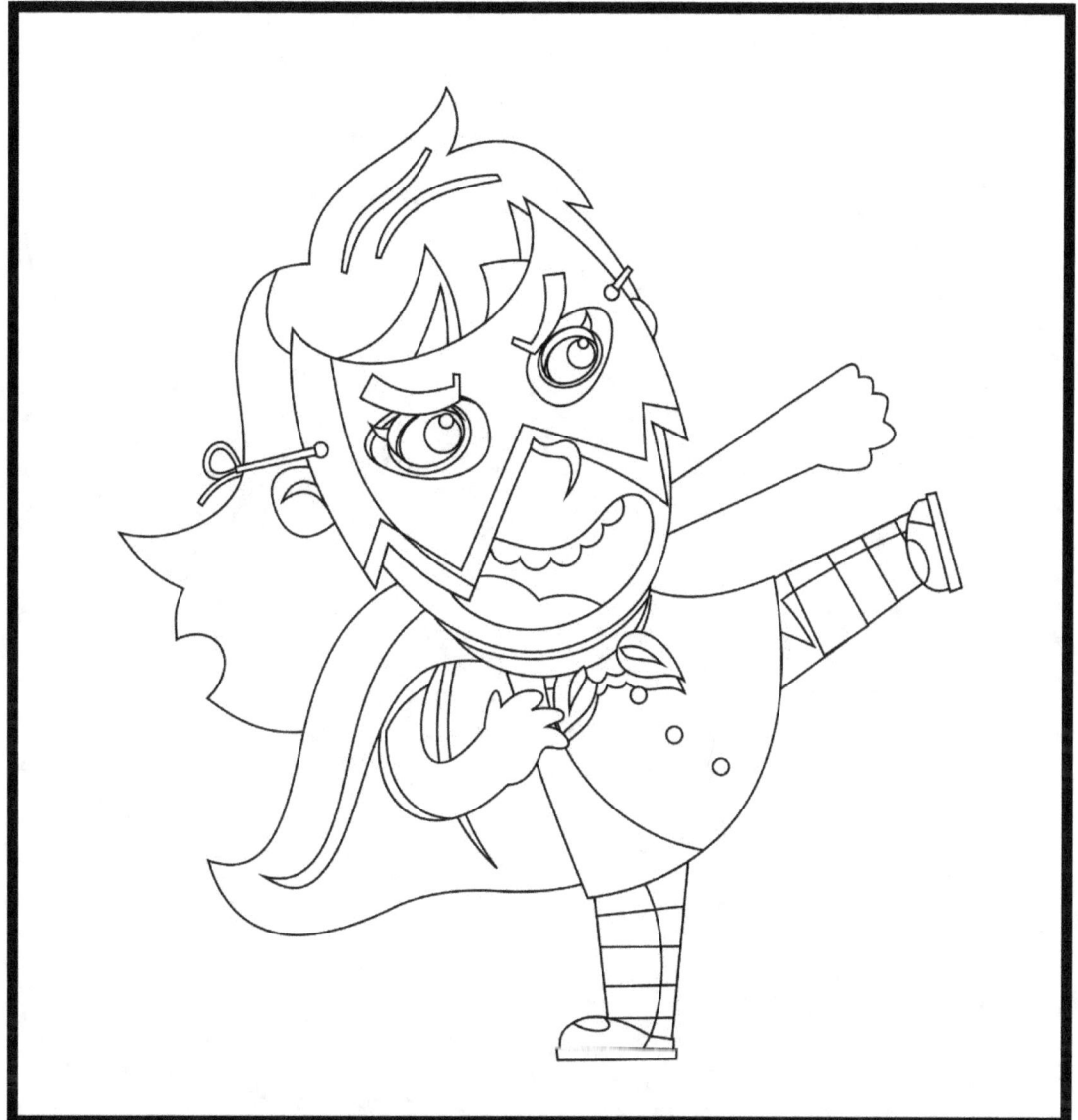

note:
_____
_____
_____

AUGUST 21TH

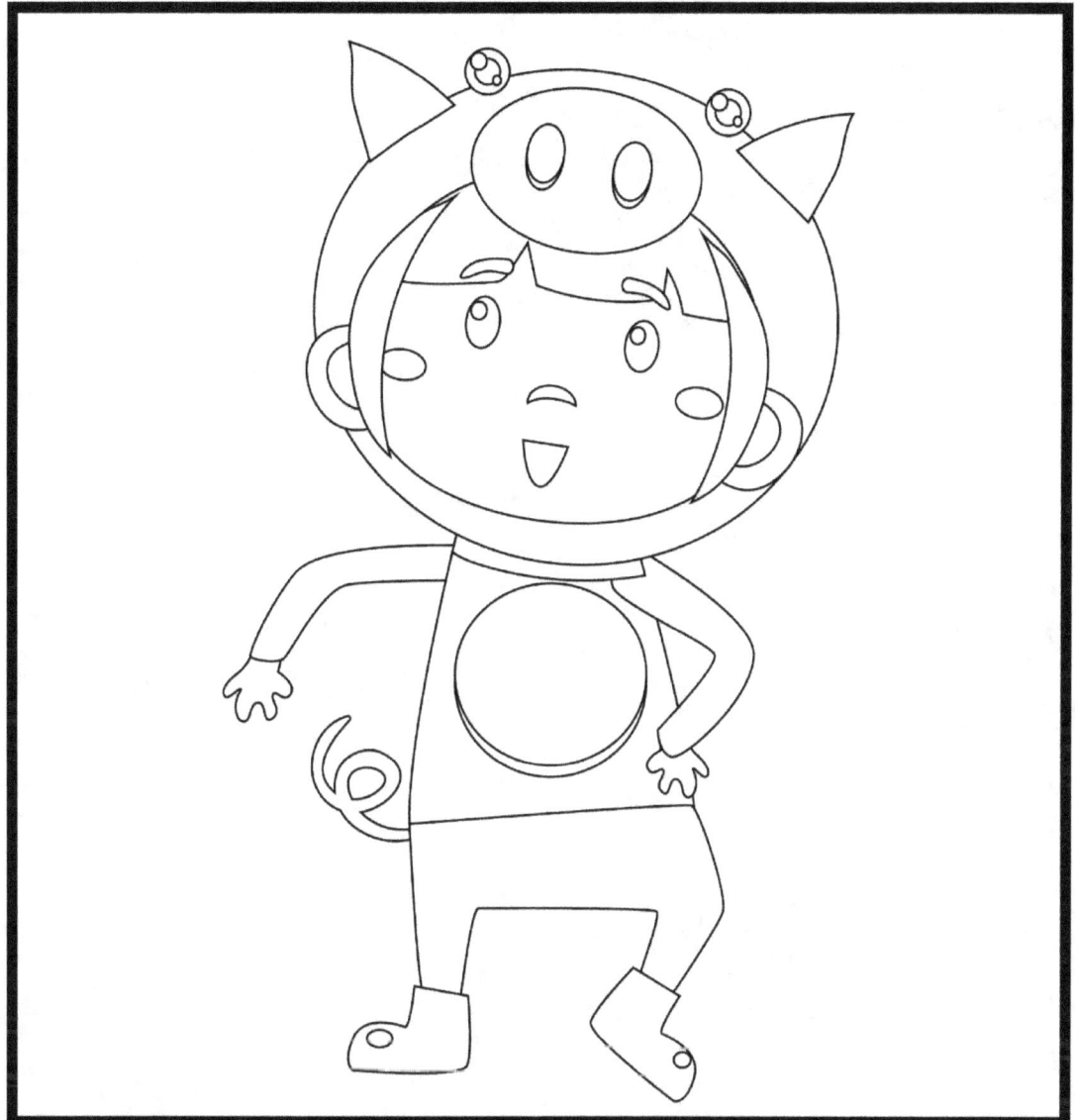

note:

_____

_____

_____

AUGUST 22TH

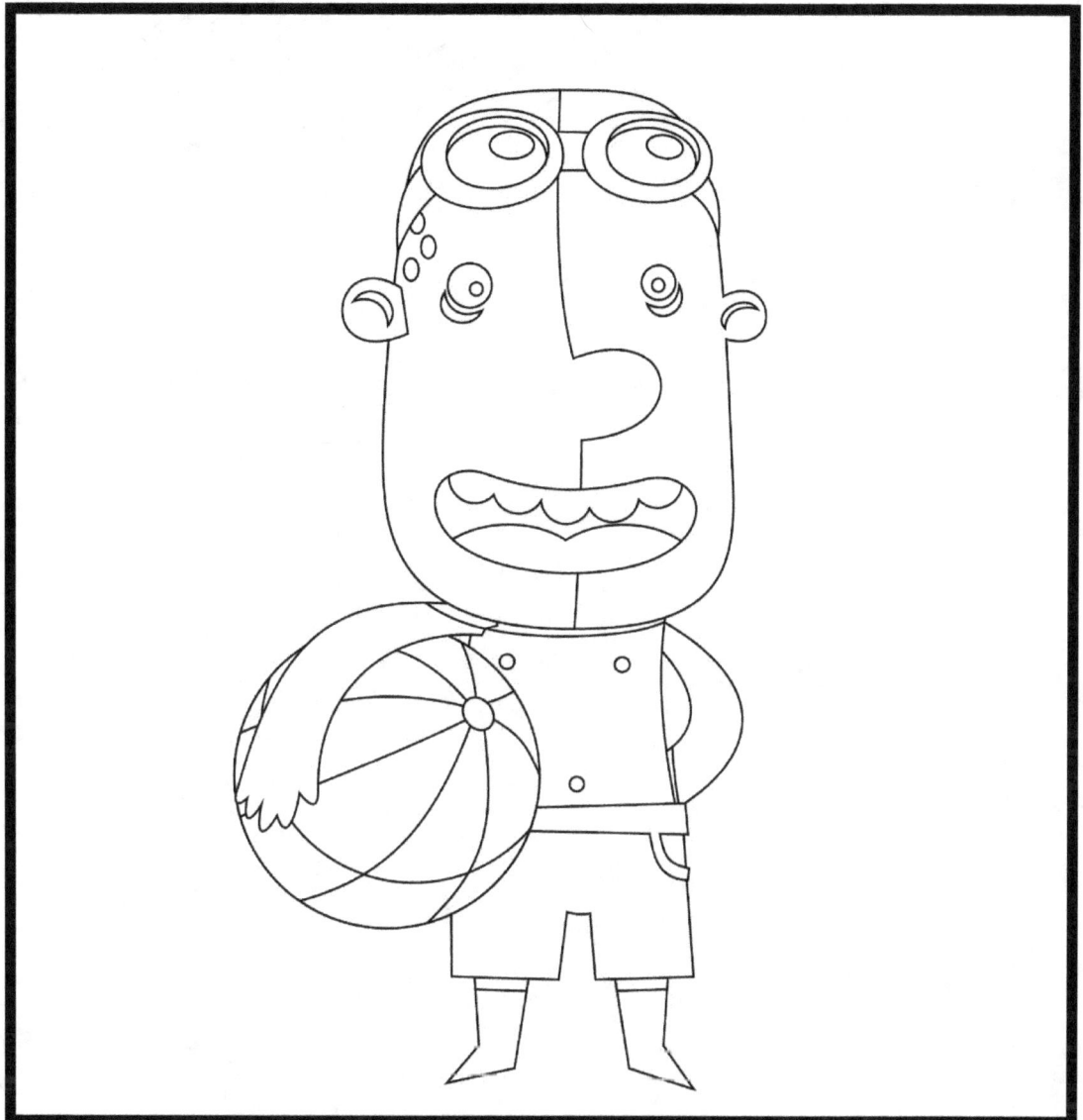

note:

_____

_____

_____

AUGUST 23TH

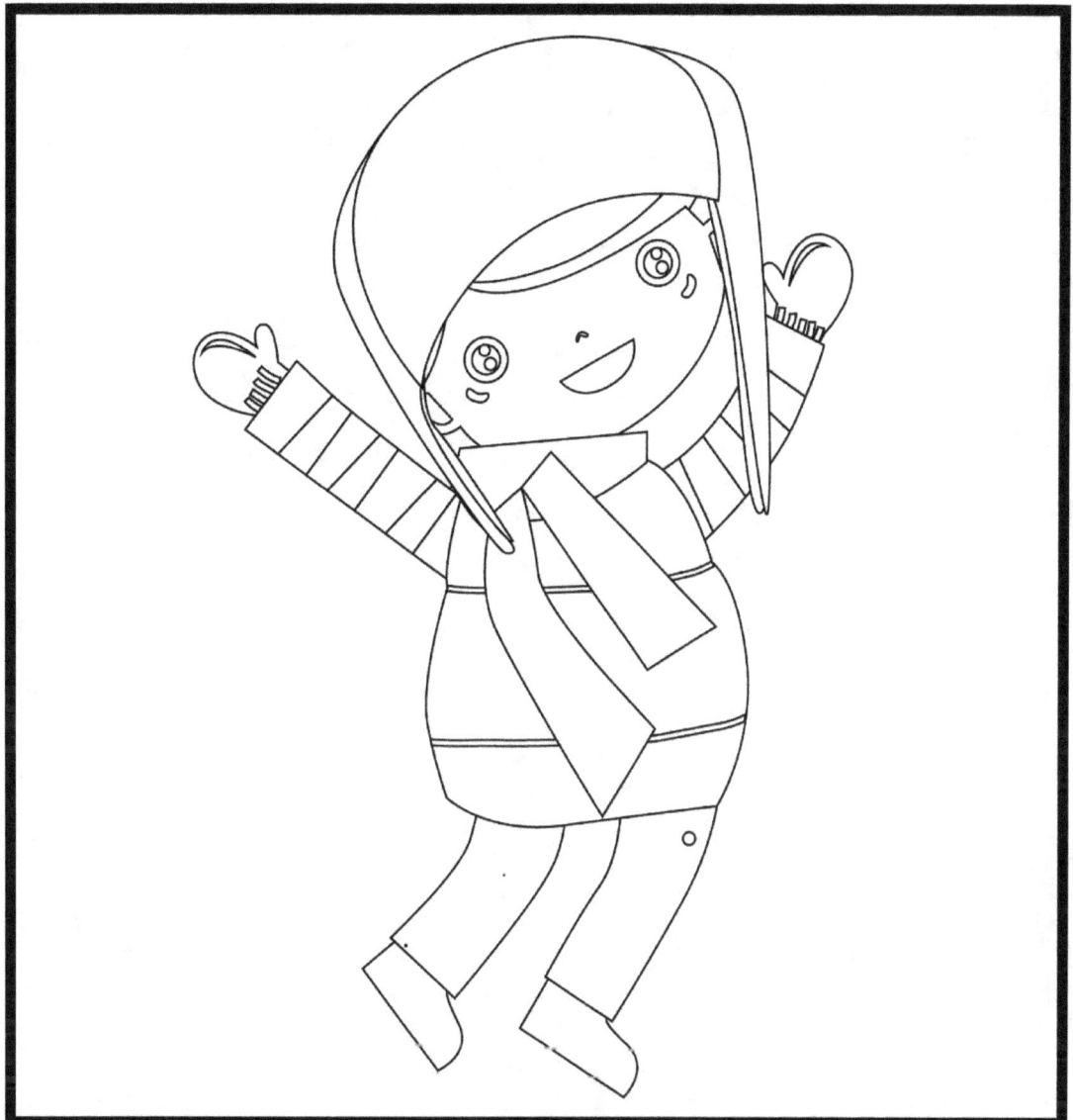

note:

_____

_____

_____

AUGUST 24TH

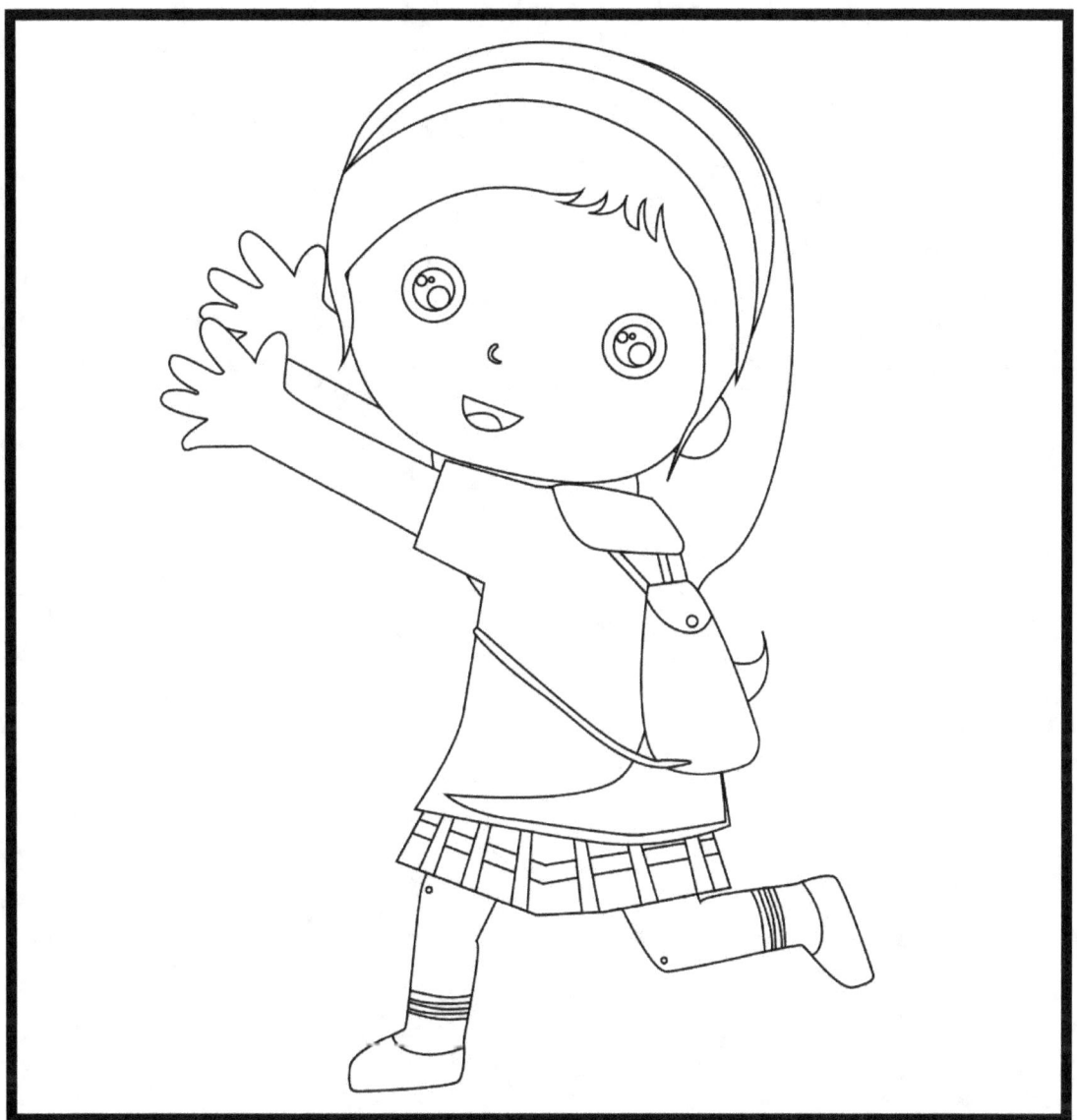

note:

_____

_____

_____

AUGUST 25TH

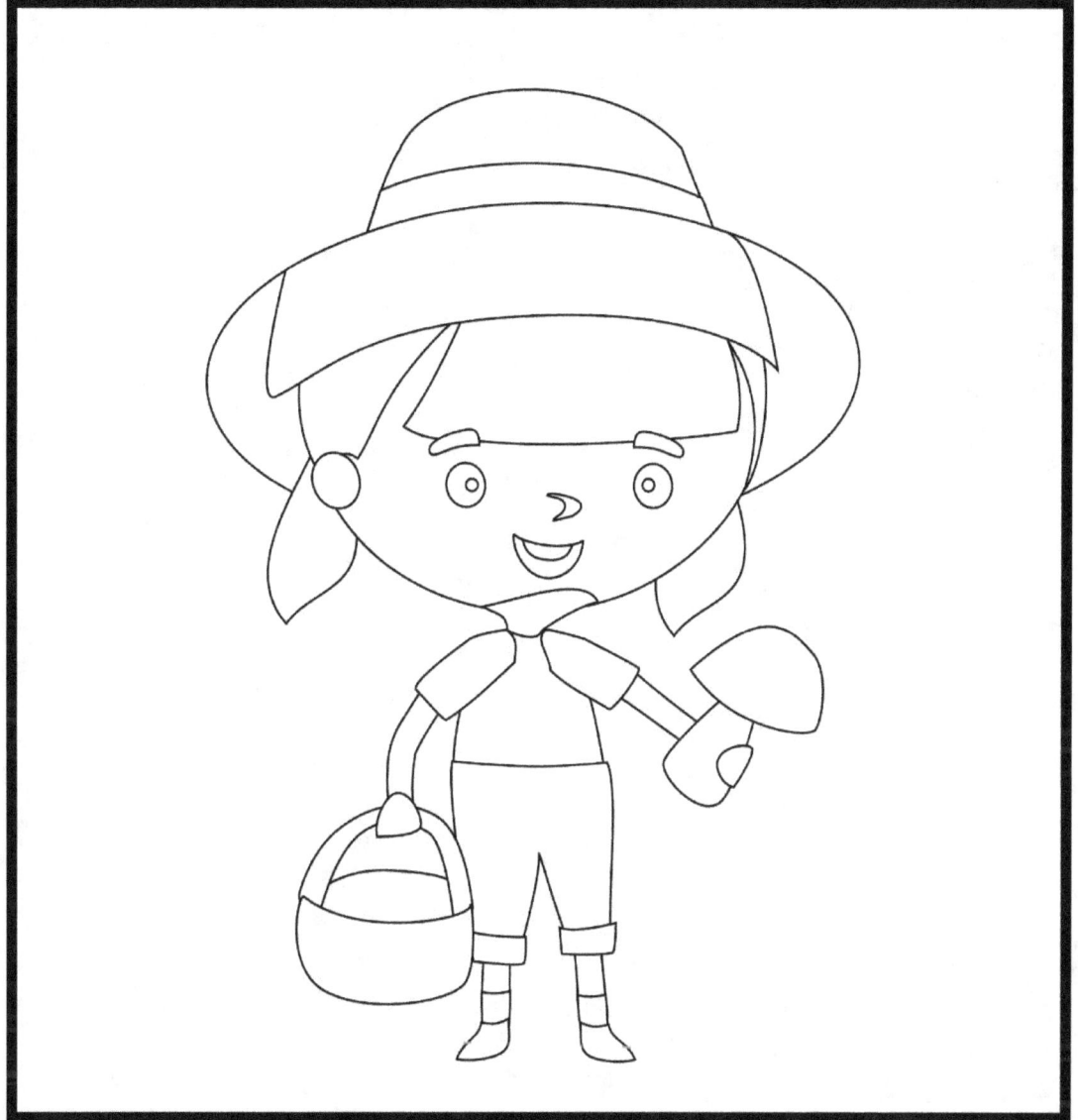

note:

_____

_____

_____

AUGUST 26TH

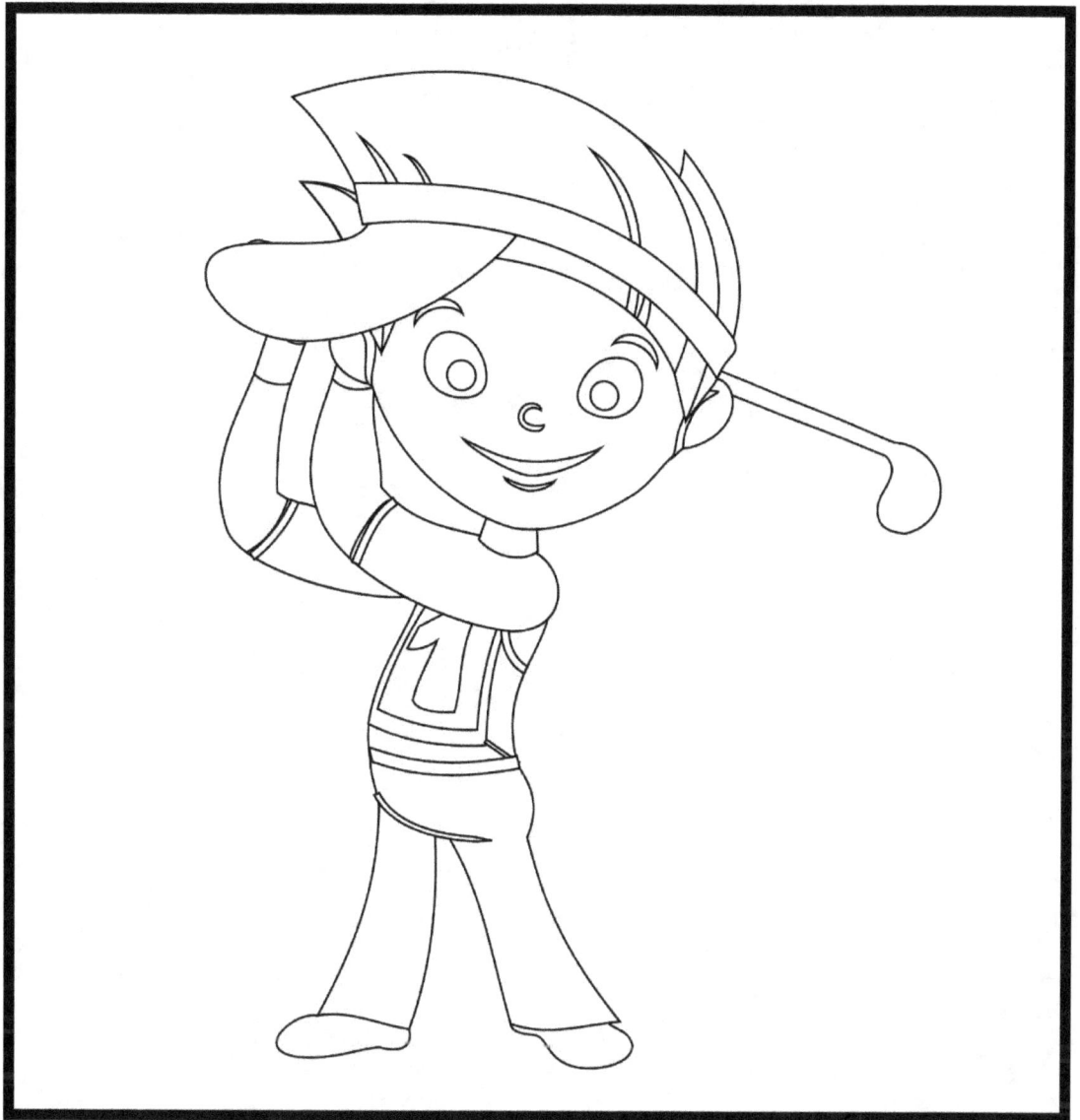

note:
_____
_____
_____

AUGUST 27TH

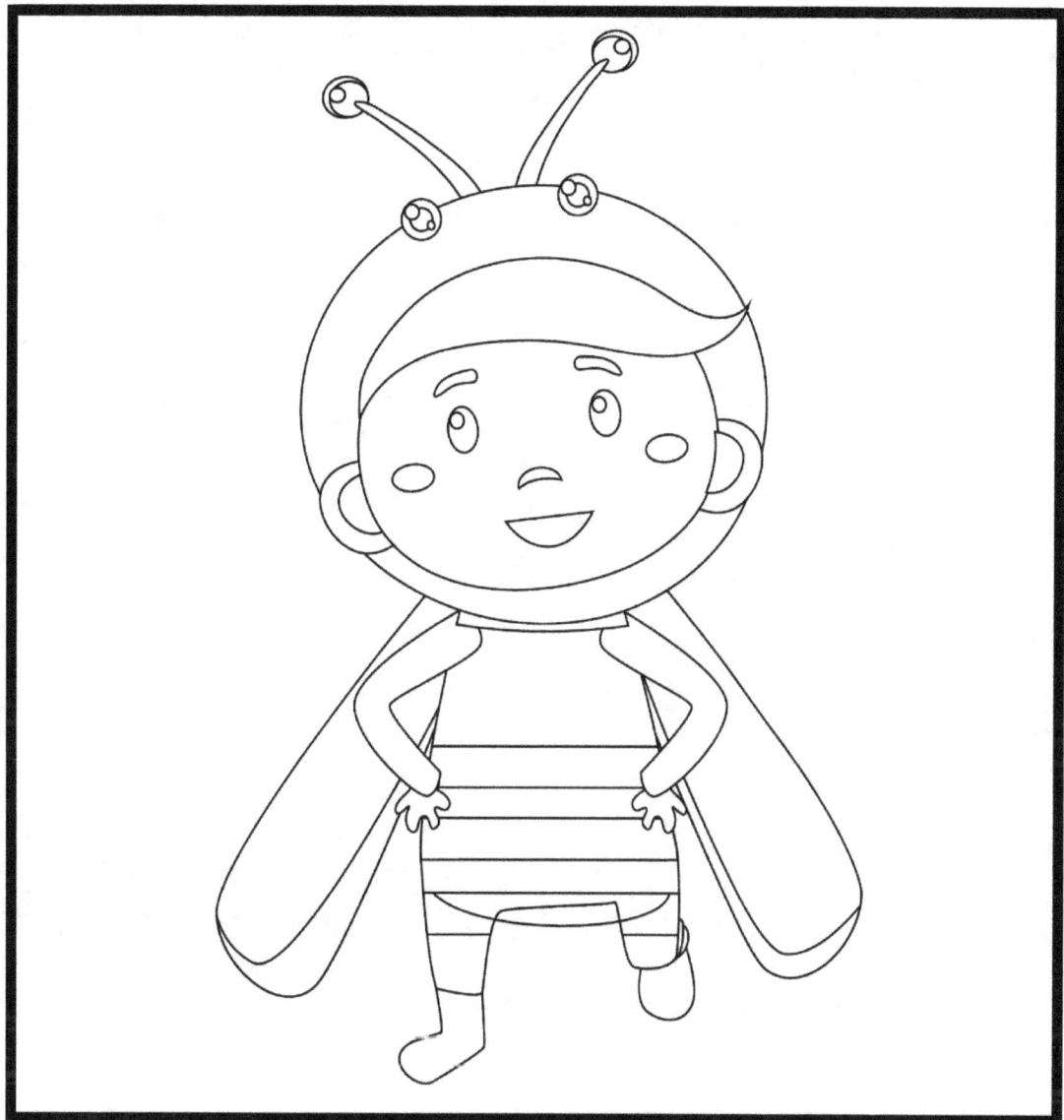

note:

_____

_____

_____

AUGUST 28TH

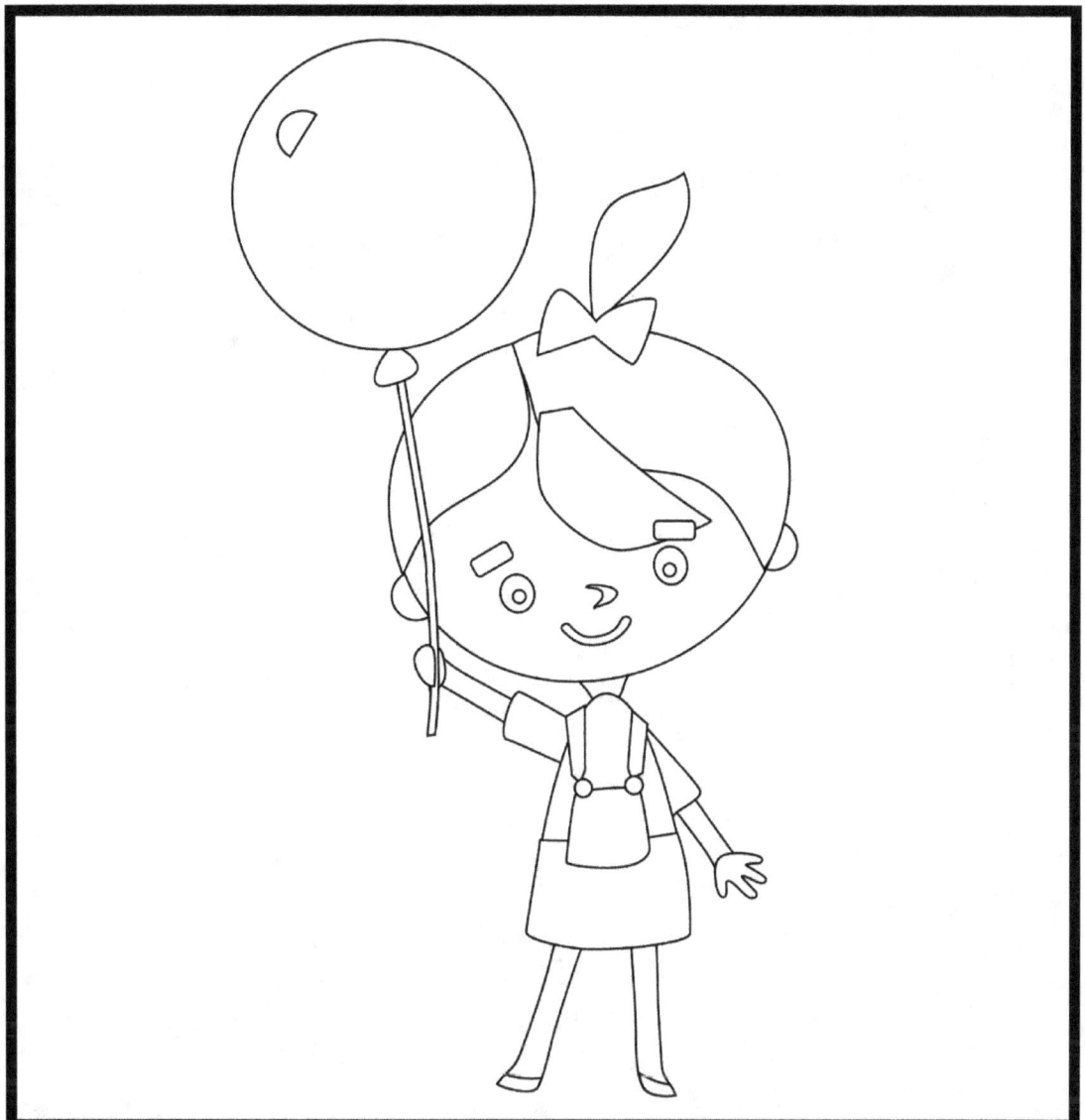

note:

_____

_____

_____

AUGUST 29TH

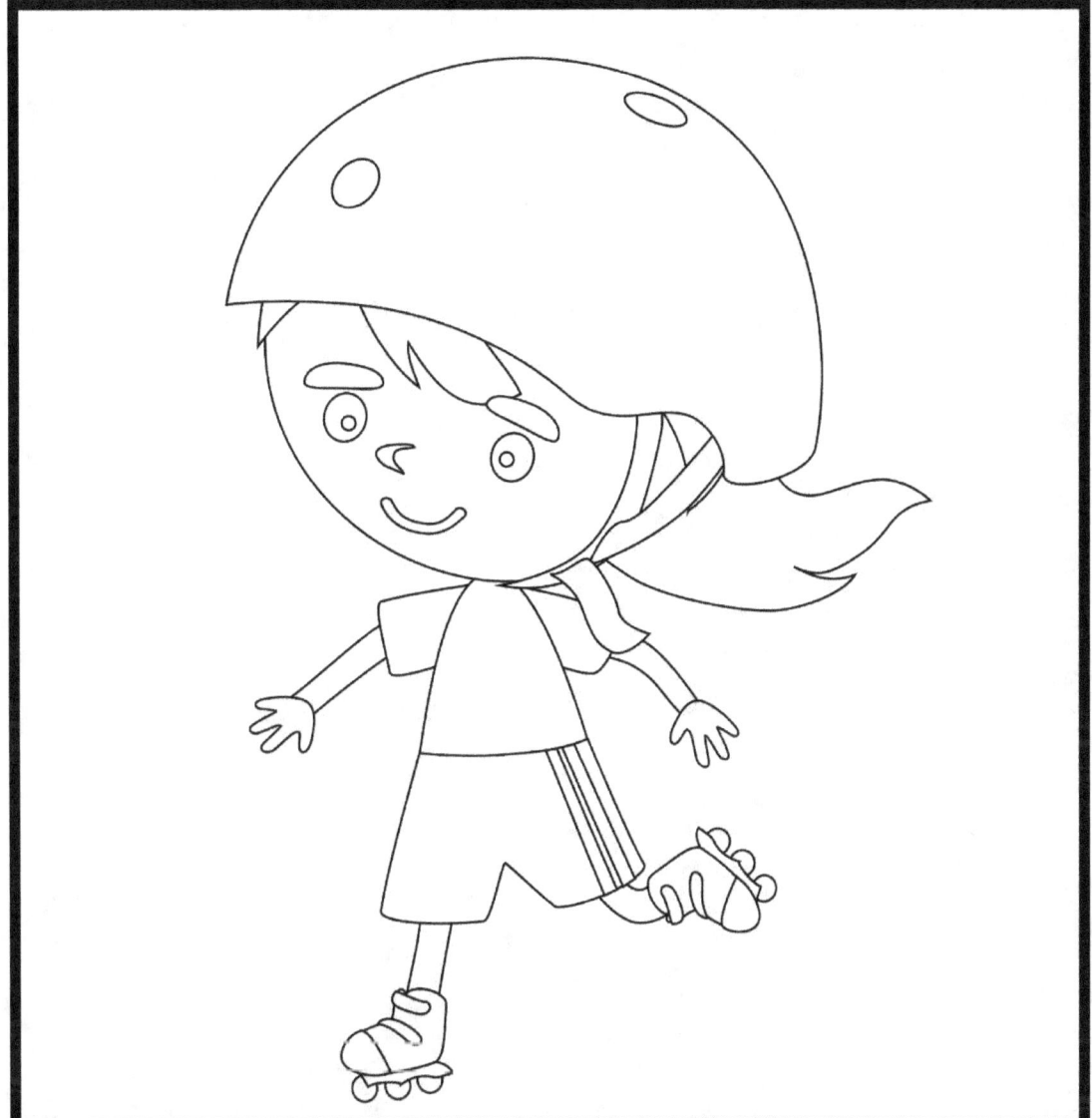

note:

_____

_____

_____

AUGUST 30TH

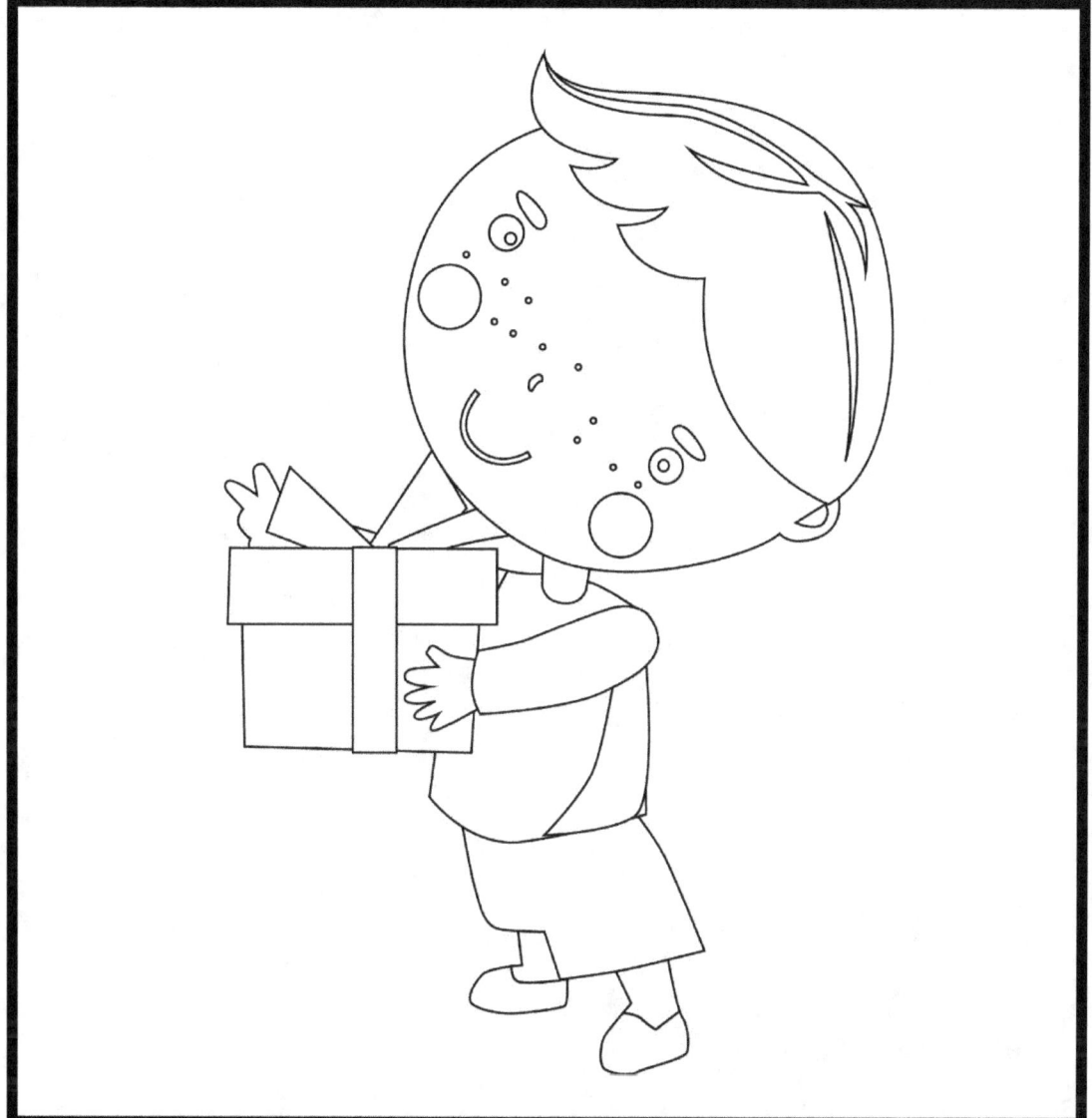

note:
_____
_____
_____

AUGUST 31TH

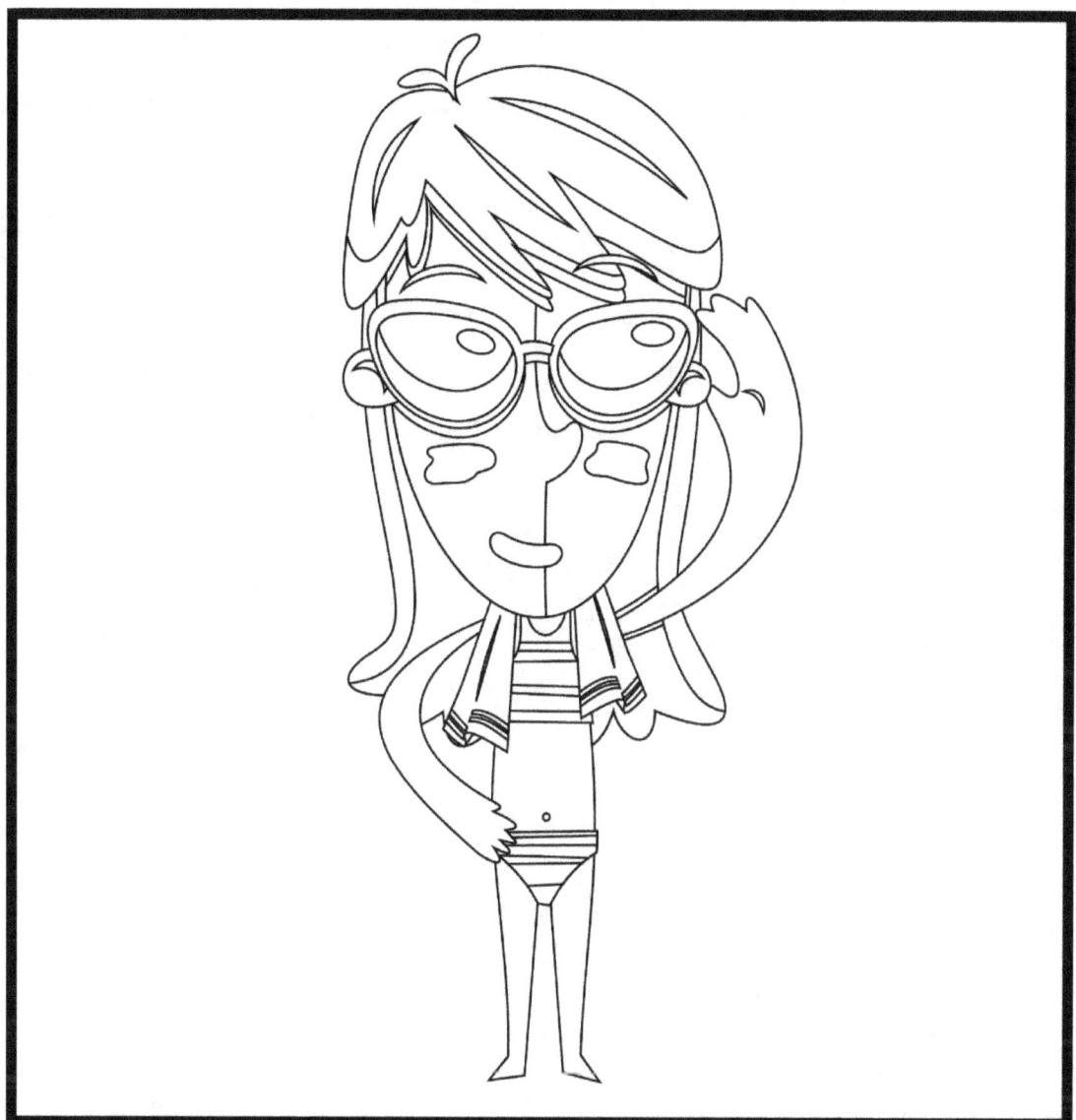

note:

_____

_____

_____

AUGUST 32TH

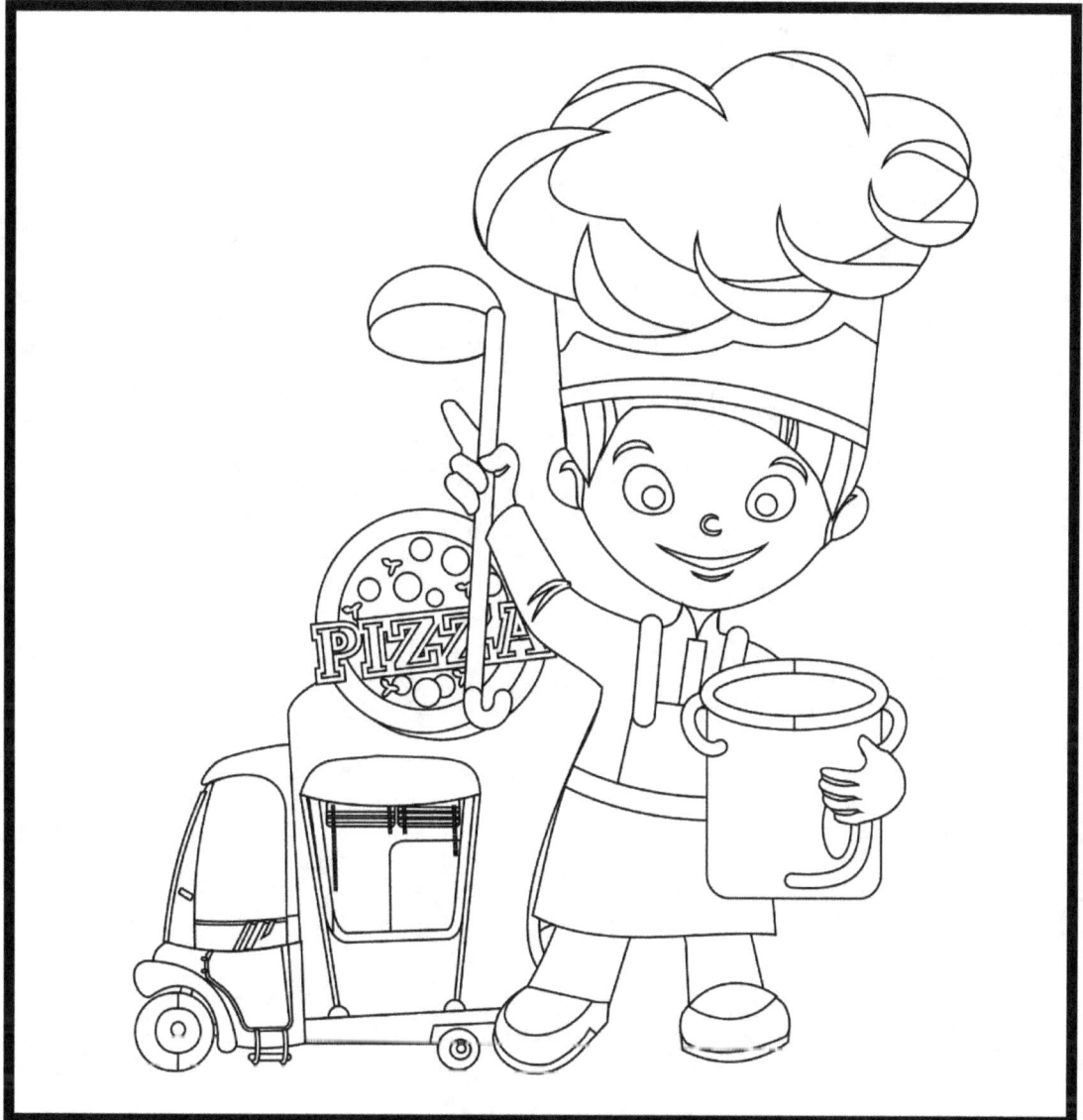

note:

_____

_____

_____

AUGUST 33TH

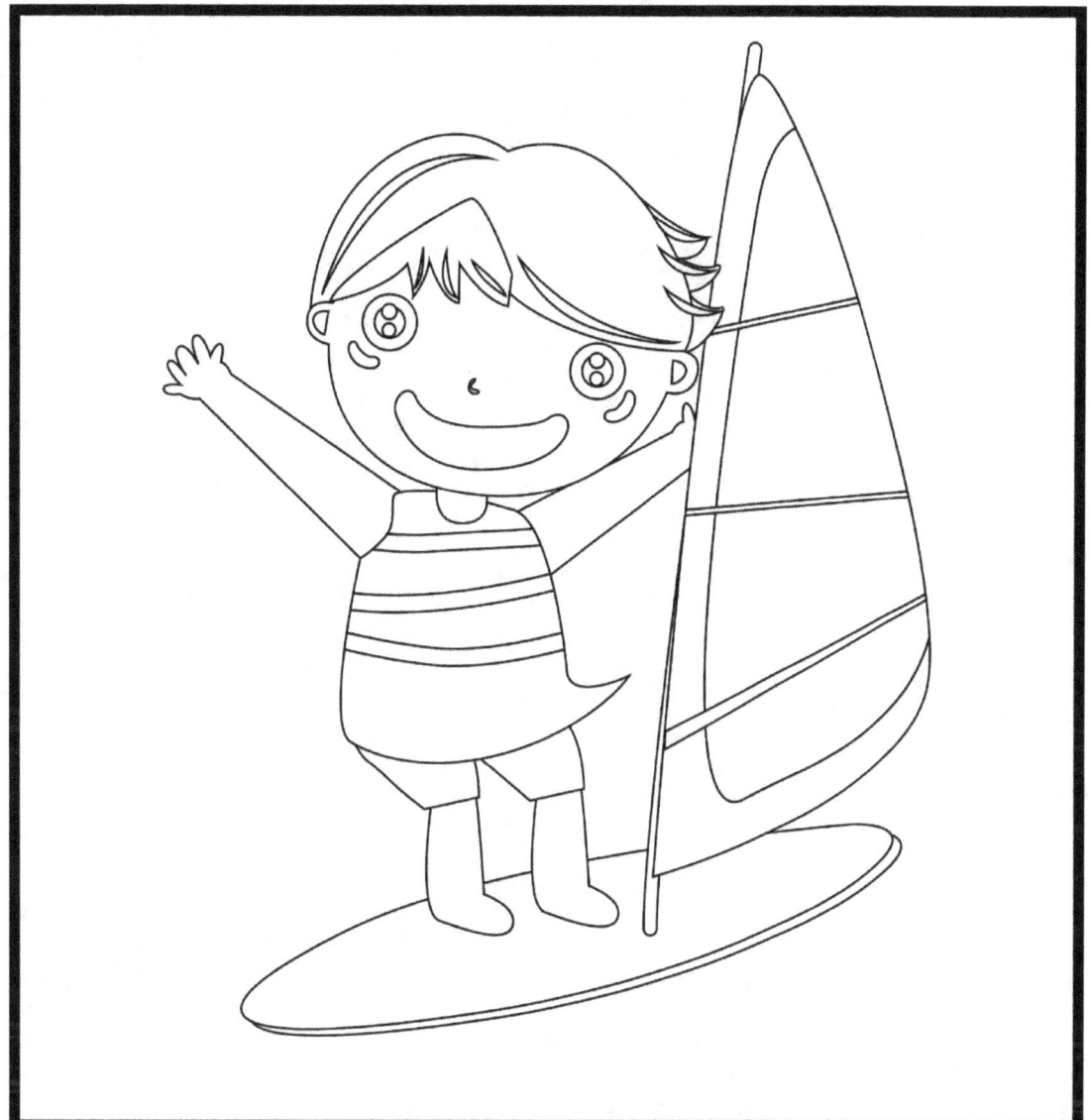

note:

_____

_____

_____

AUGUST 34TH

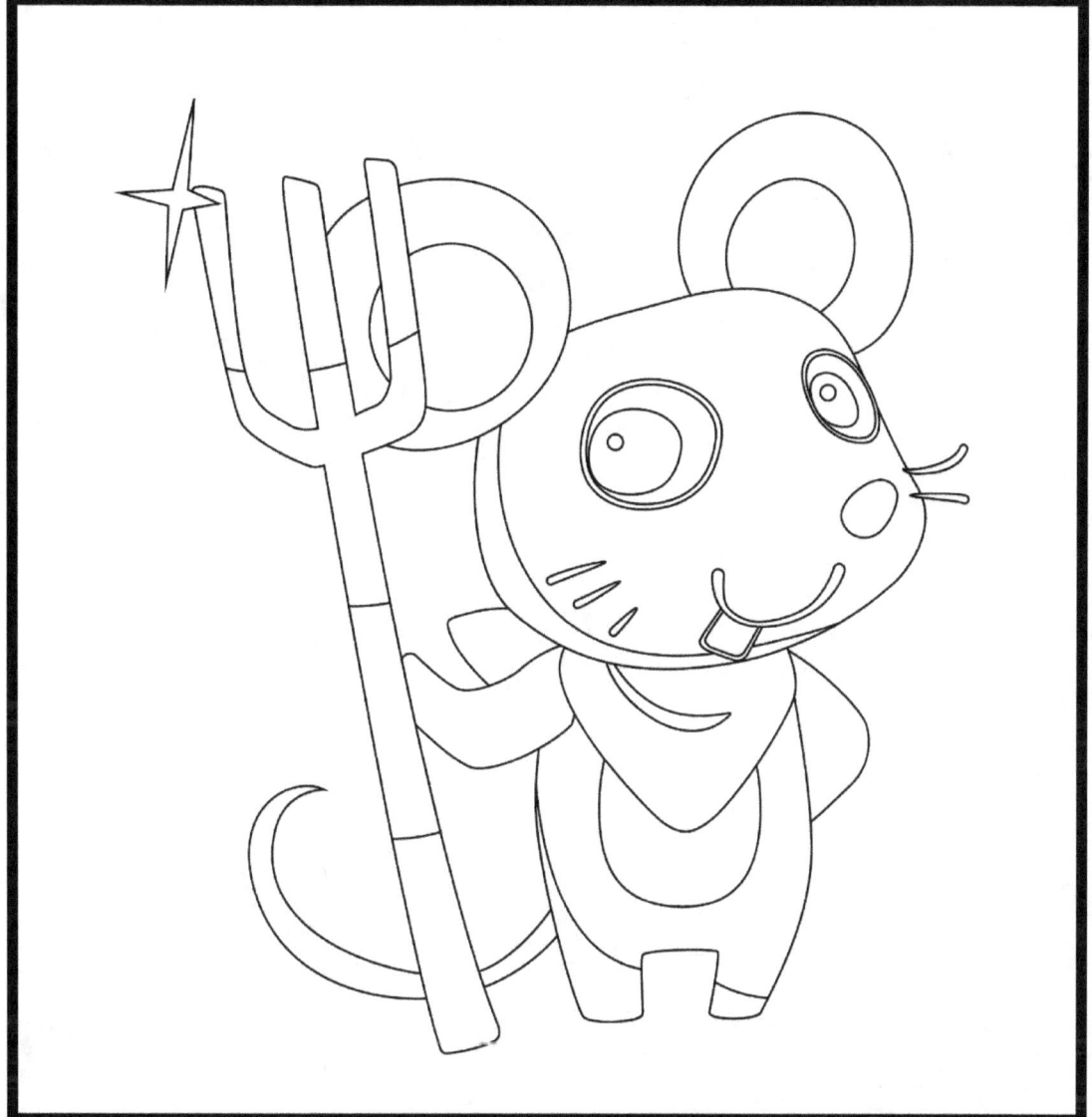

note:

_____

_____

_____

AUGUST 35TH

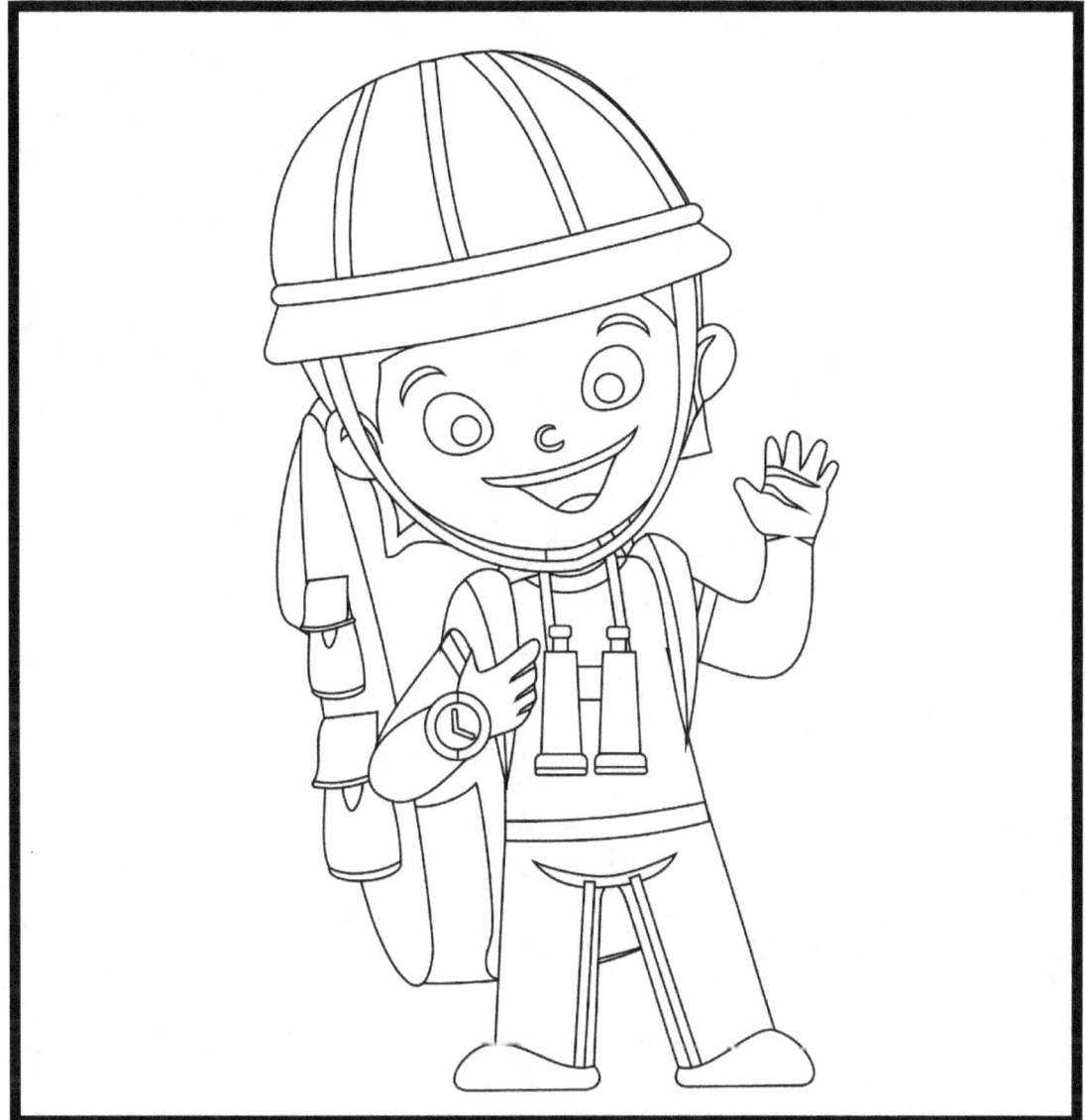

note:

_____

_____

_____

AUGUST 36TH

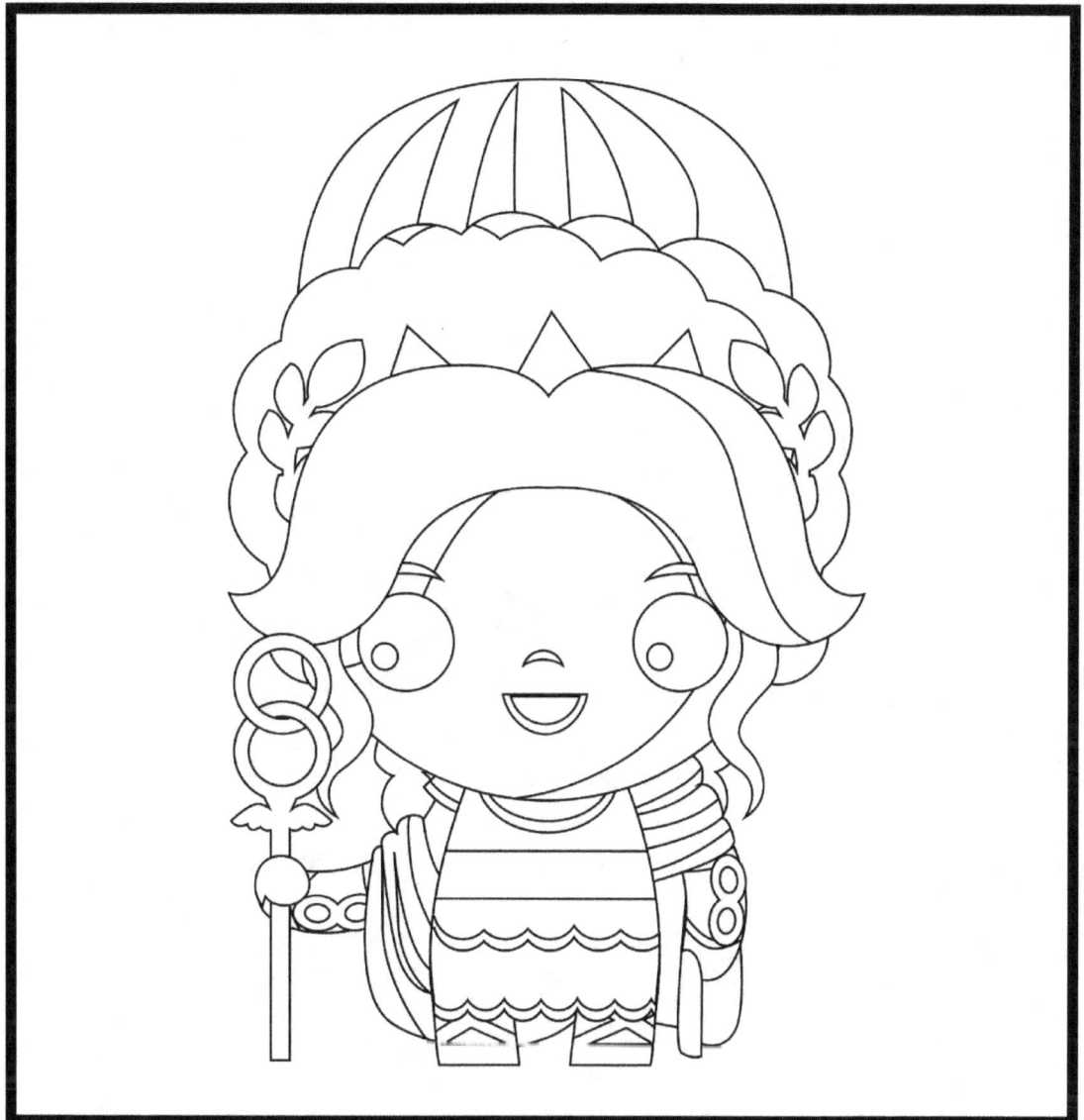

note:

_____

_____

_____

AUGUST 37TH

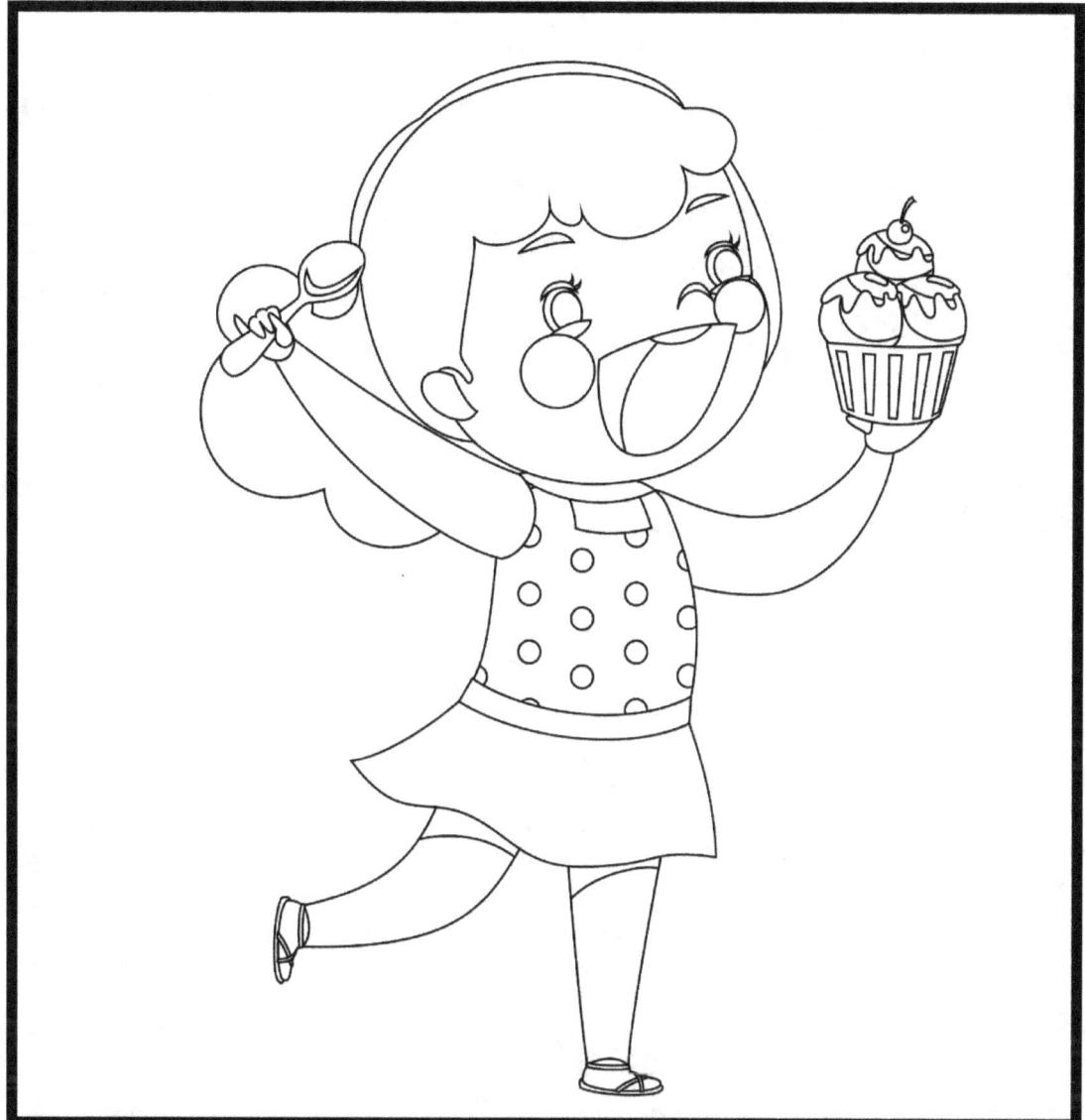

note:

_____

_____

_____

AUGUST 38TH

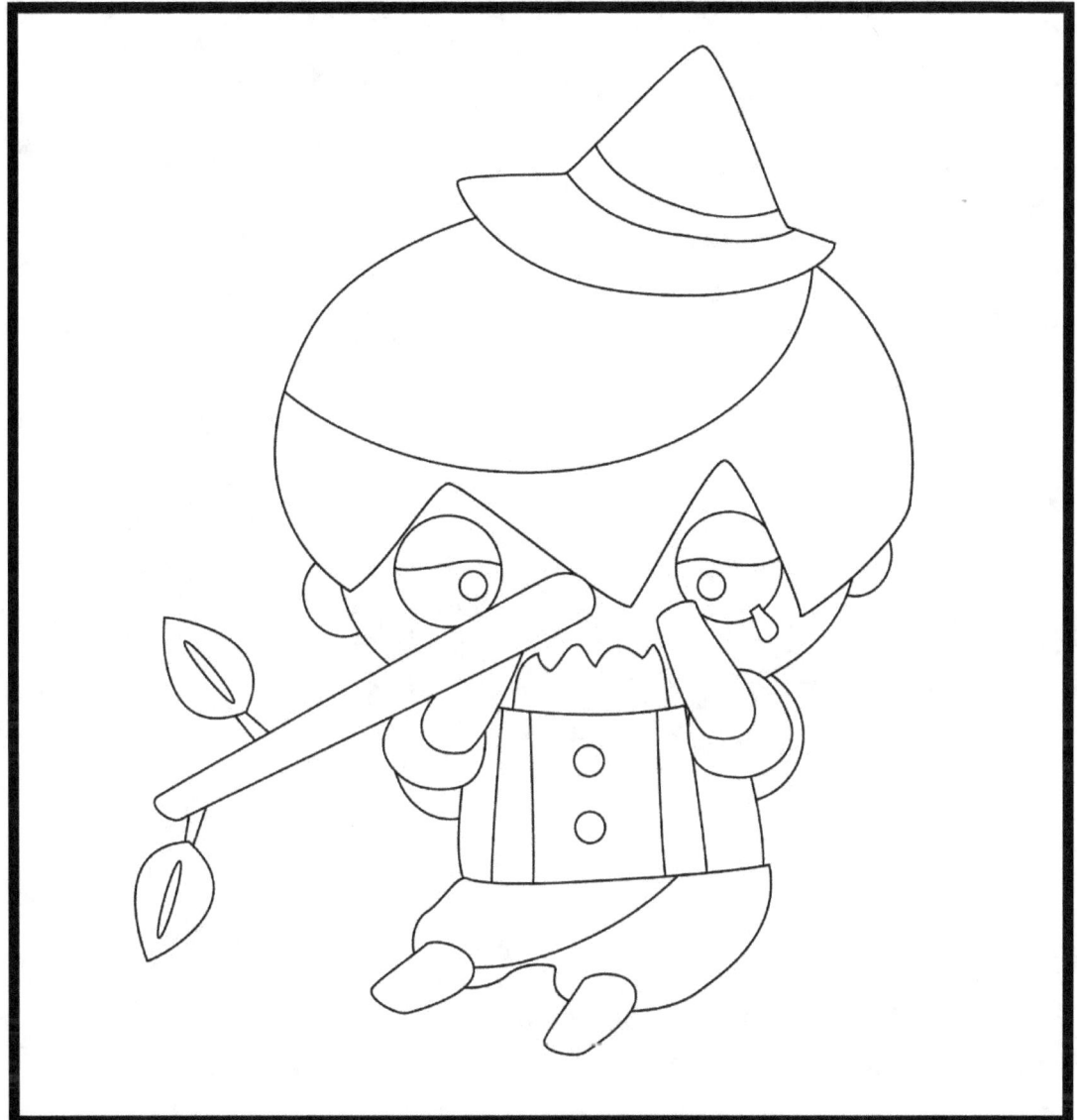

note:

_____

_____

_____

AUGUST 39TH

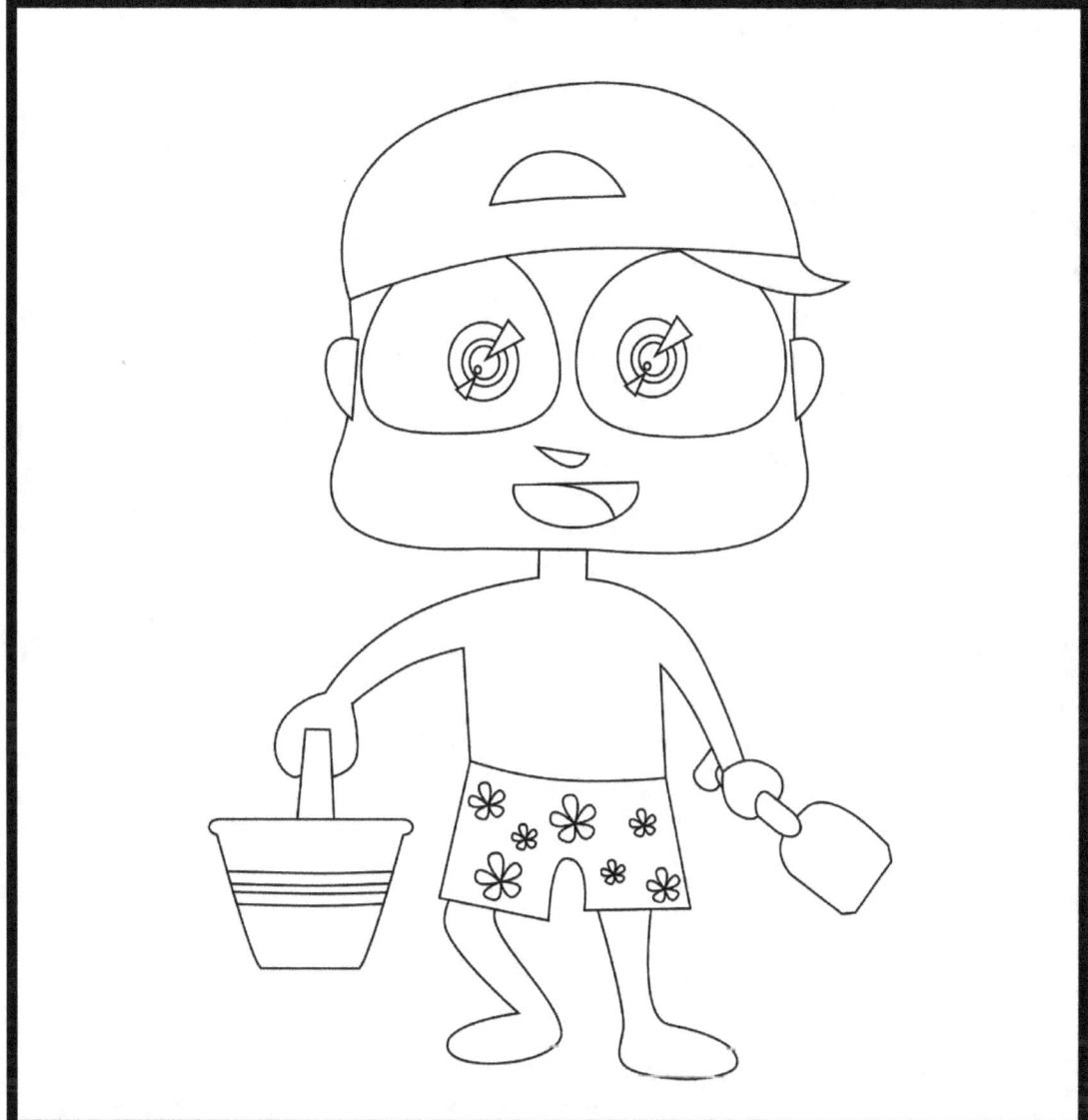

note:

_____

_____

_____

AUGUST 40TH

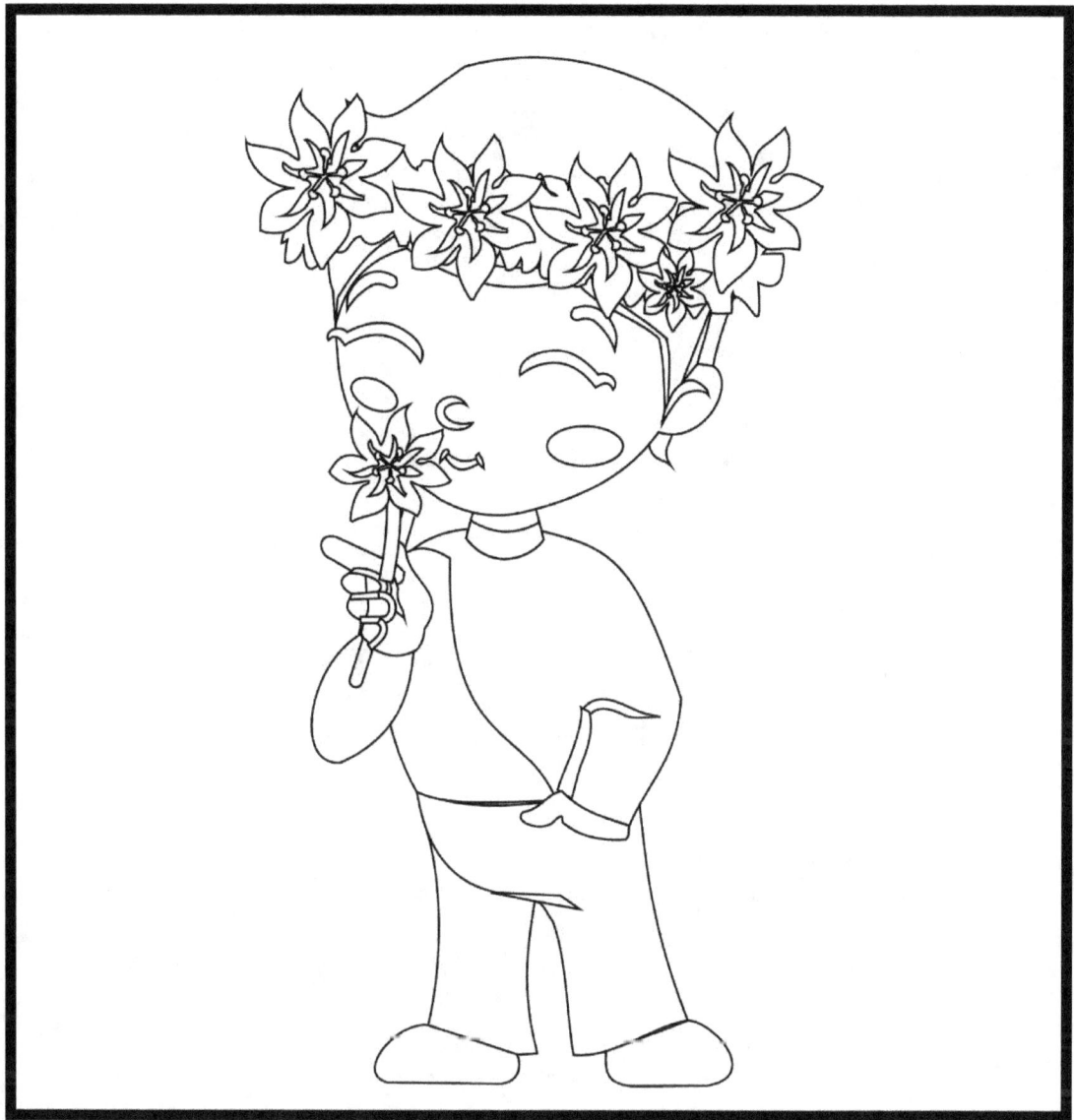

note:

_____

_____

_____

AUGUST 41TH

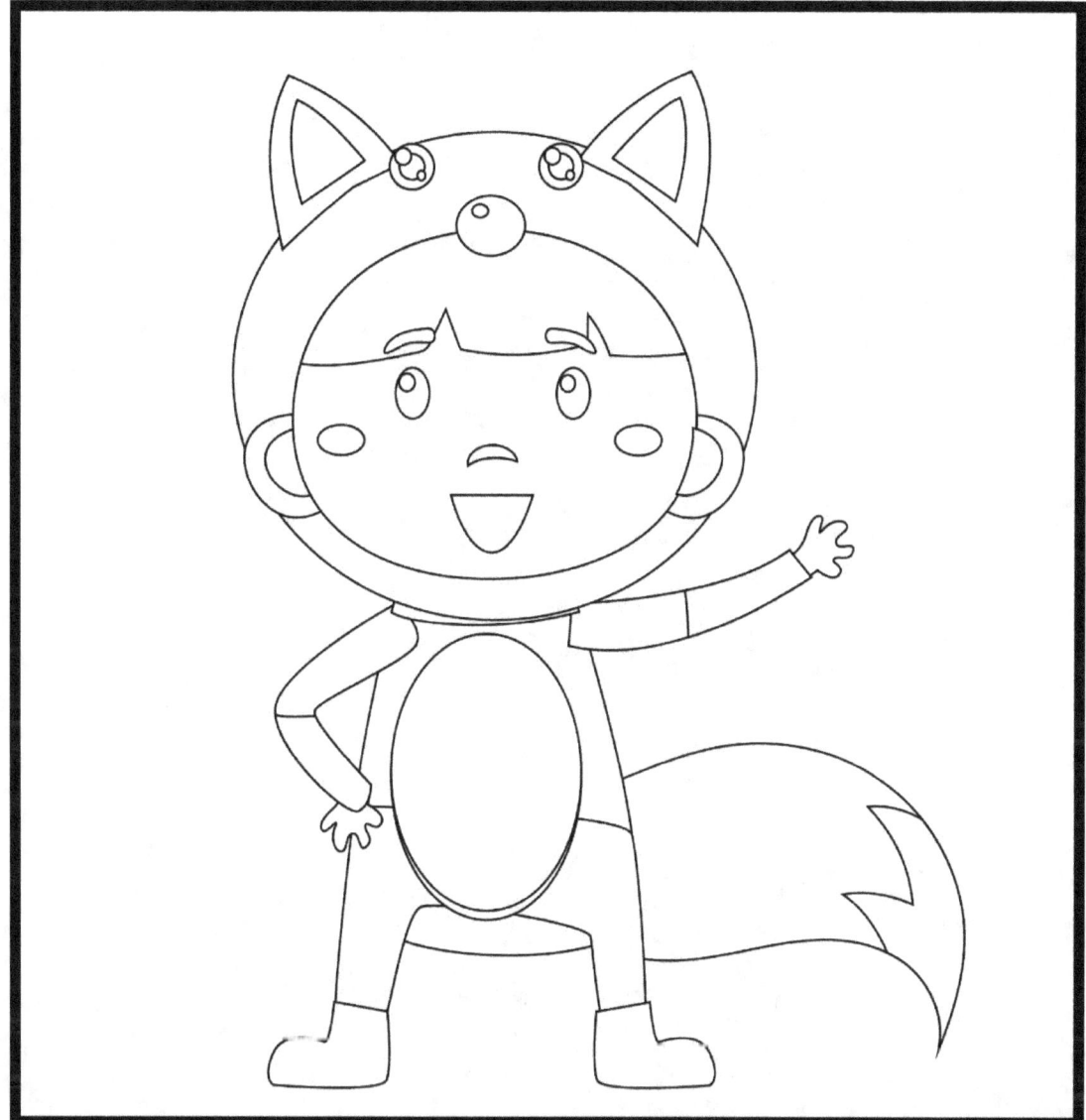

note:

_____

_____

_____

AUGUST 42TH

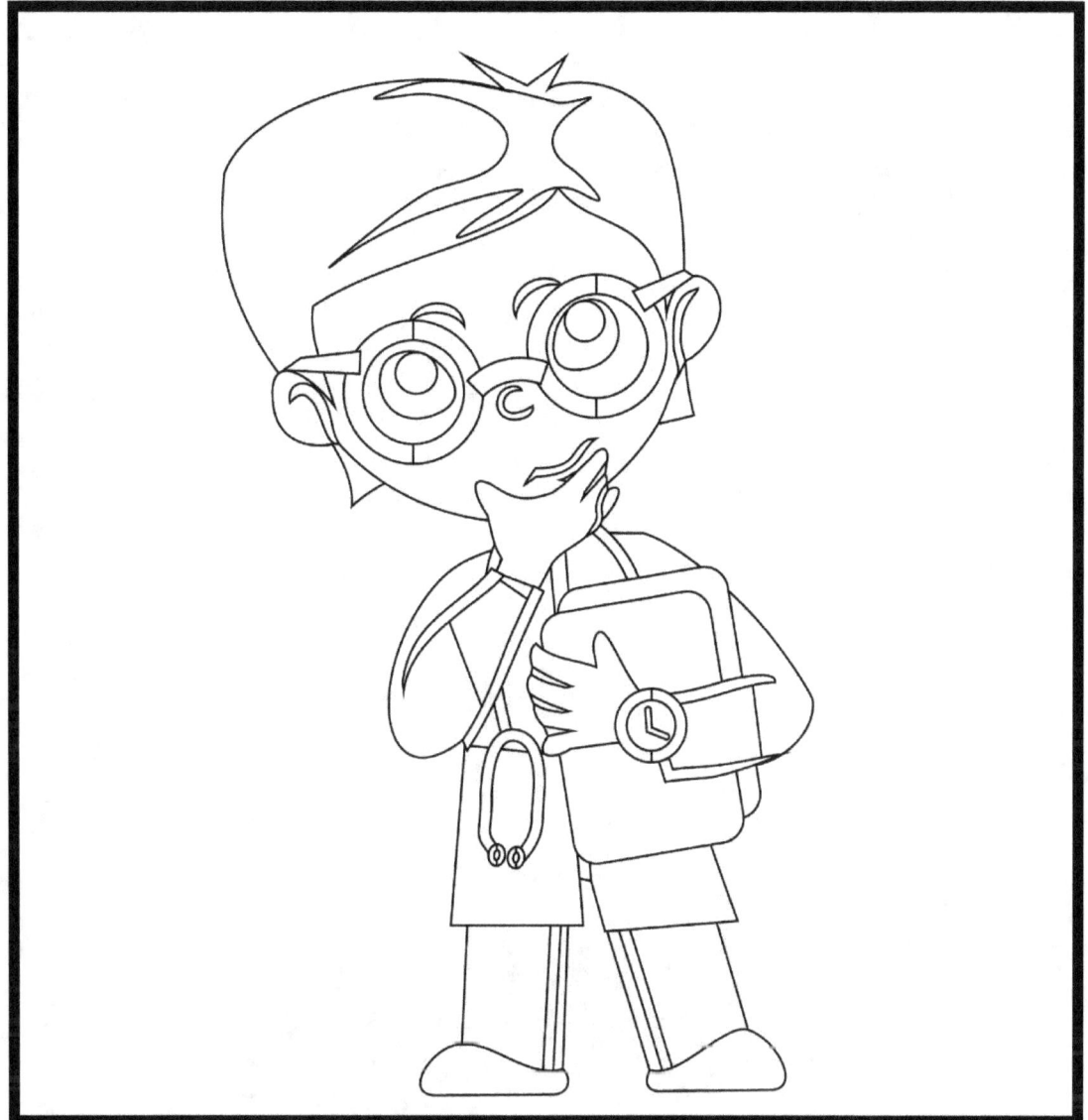

note:

_____

_____

_____

AUGUST 43TH

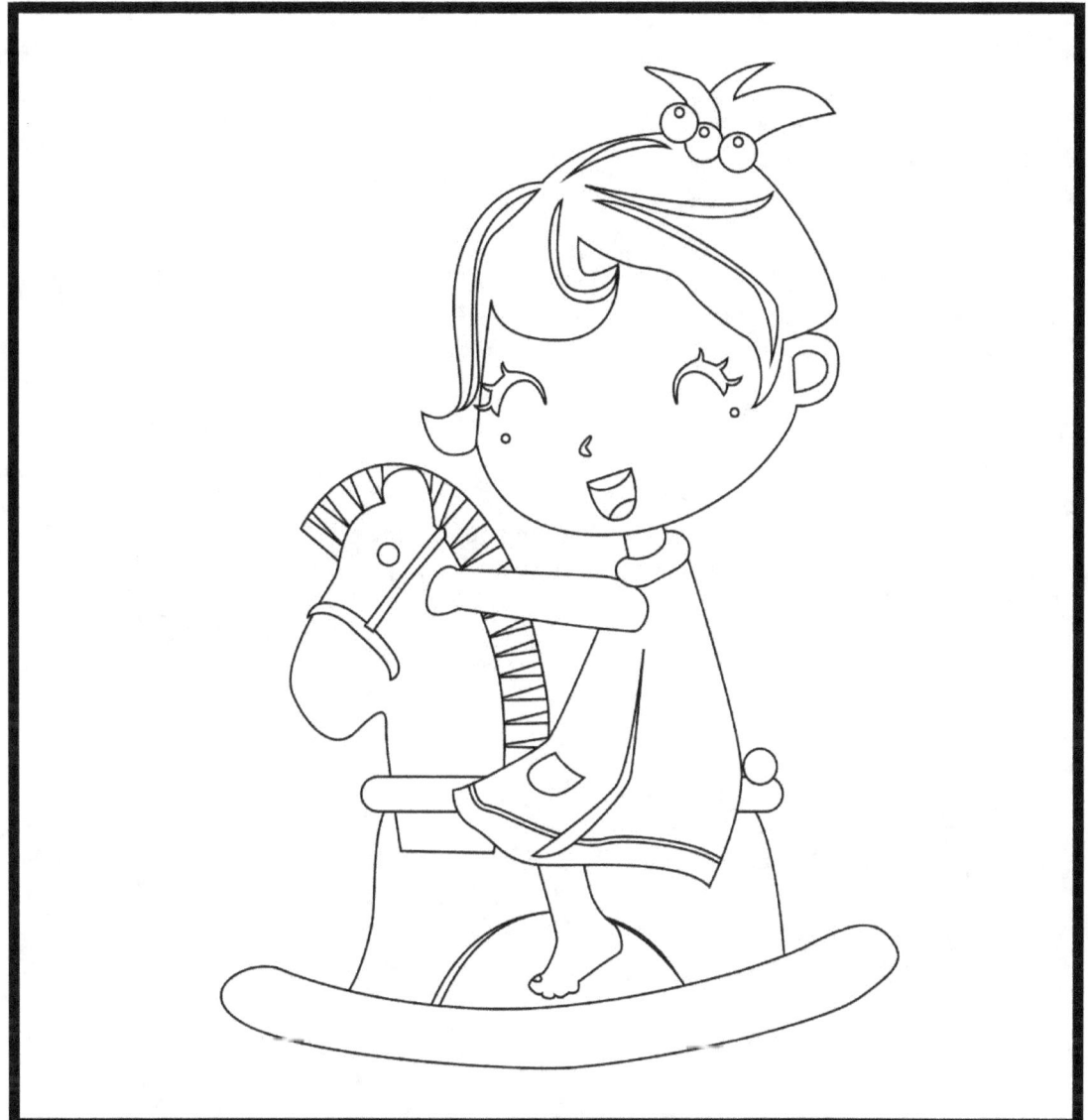

note:

_____

_____

_____

AUGUST 44TH

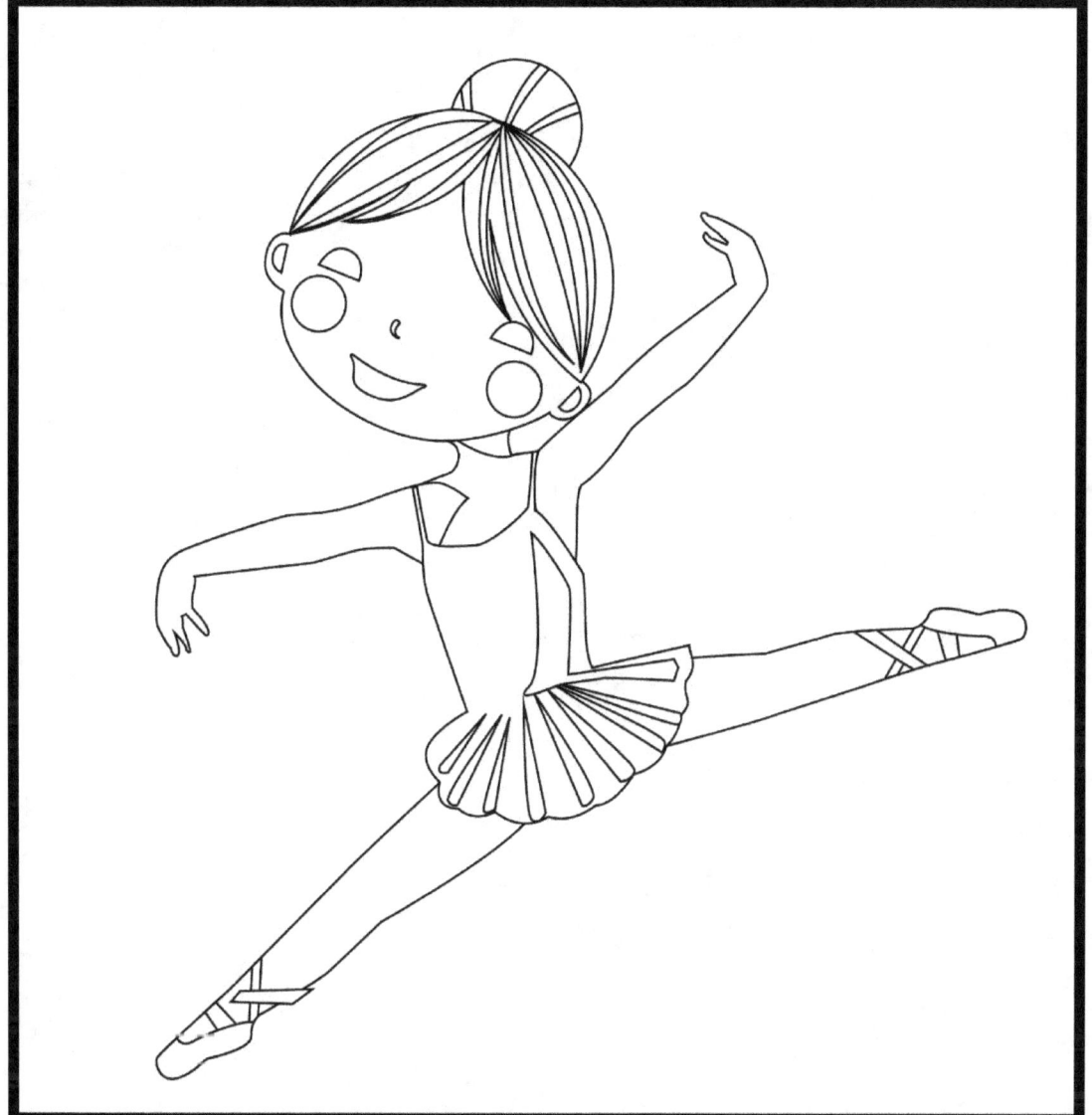

note:

_____

_____

_____

AUGUST 45TH

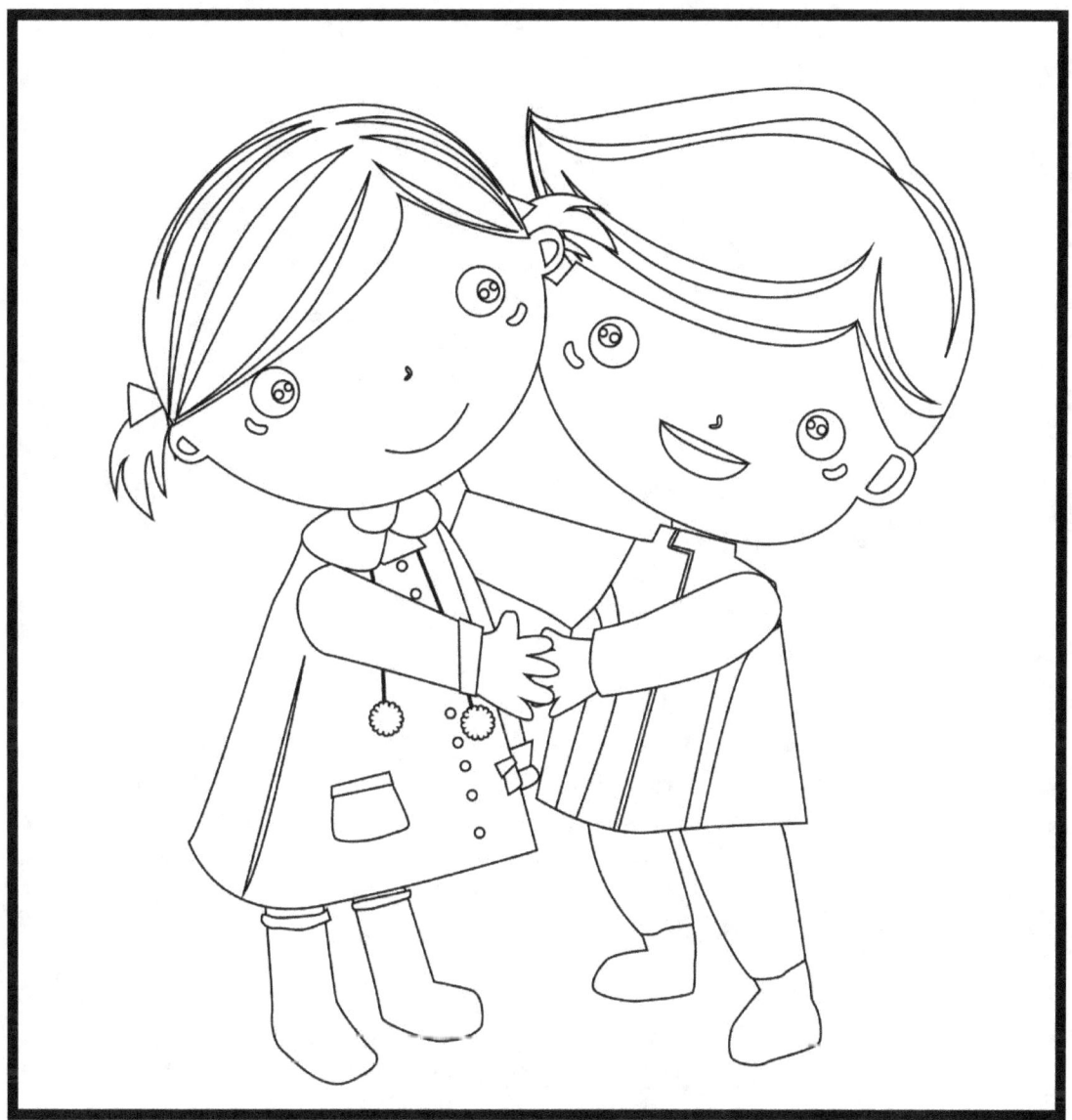

note:

_____

_____

_____

AUGUST 46TH

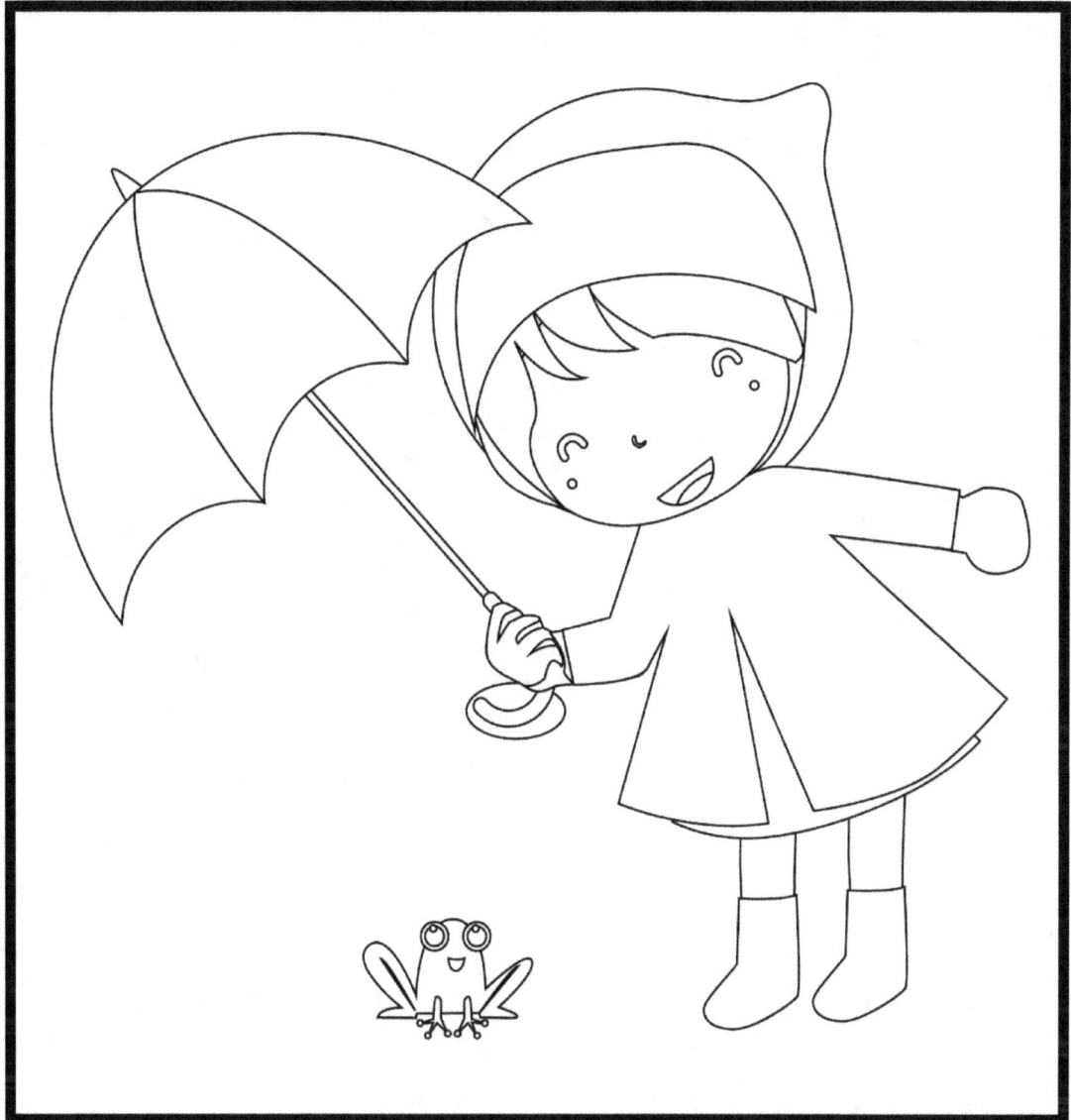

note:

_____

_____

_____

AUGUST 47TH

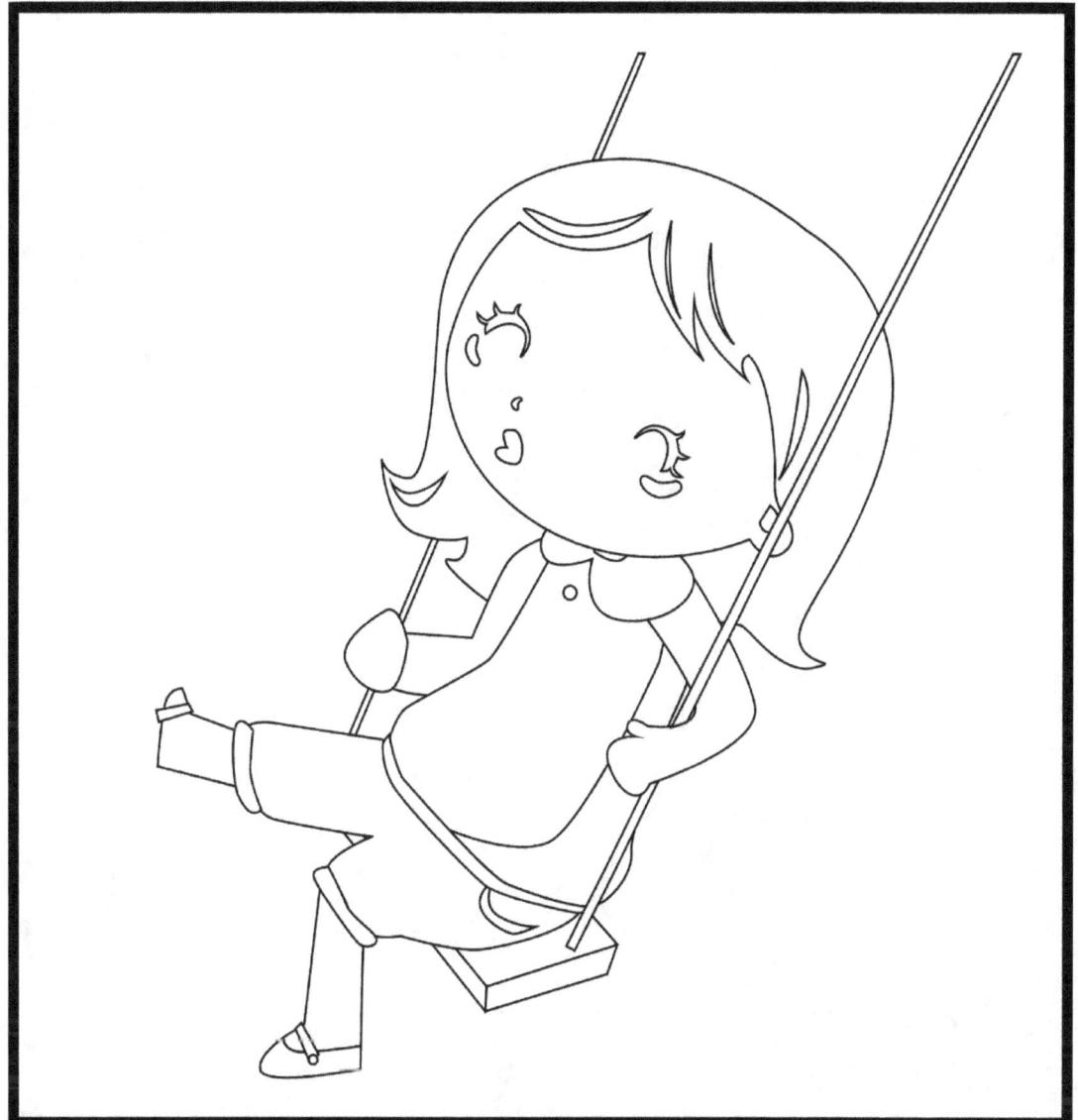

note:

_____

_____

_____

AUGUST 48TH

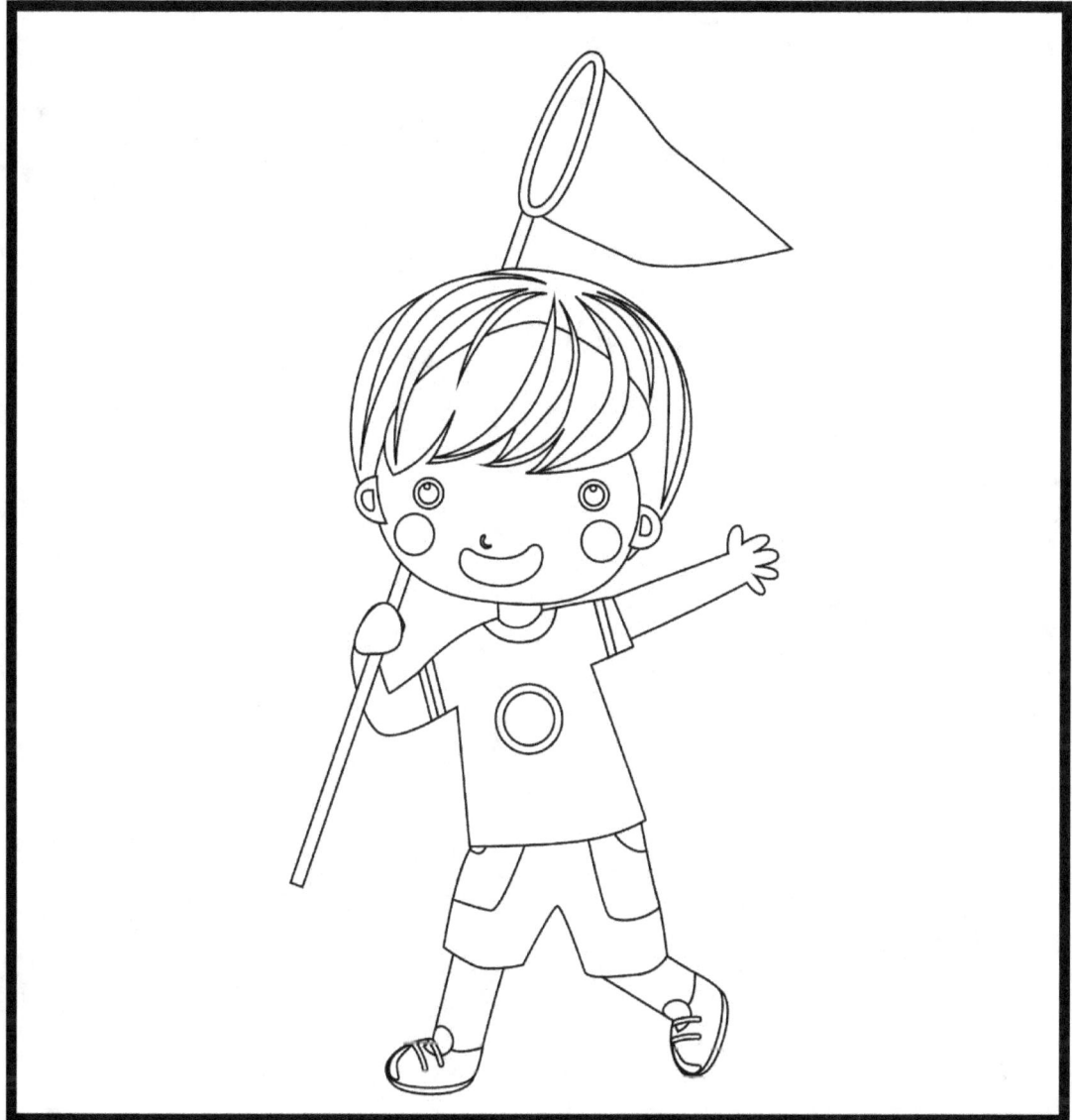

note:

_____

_____

_____

AUGUST 49TH

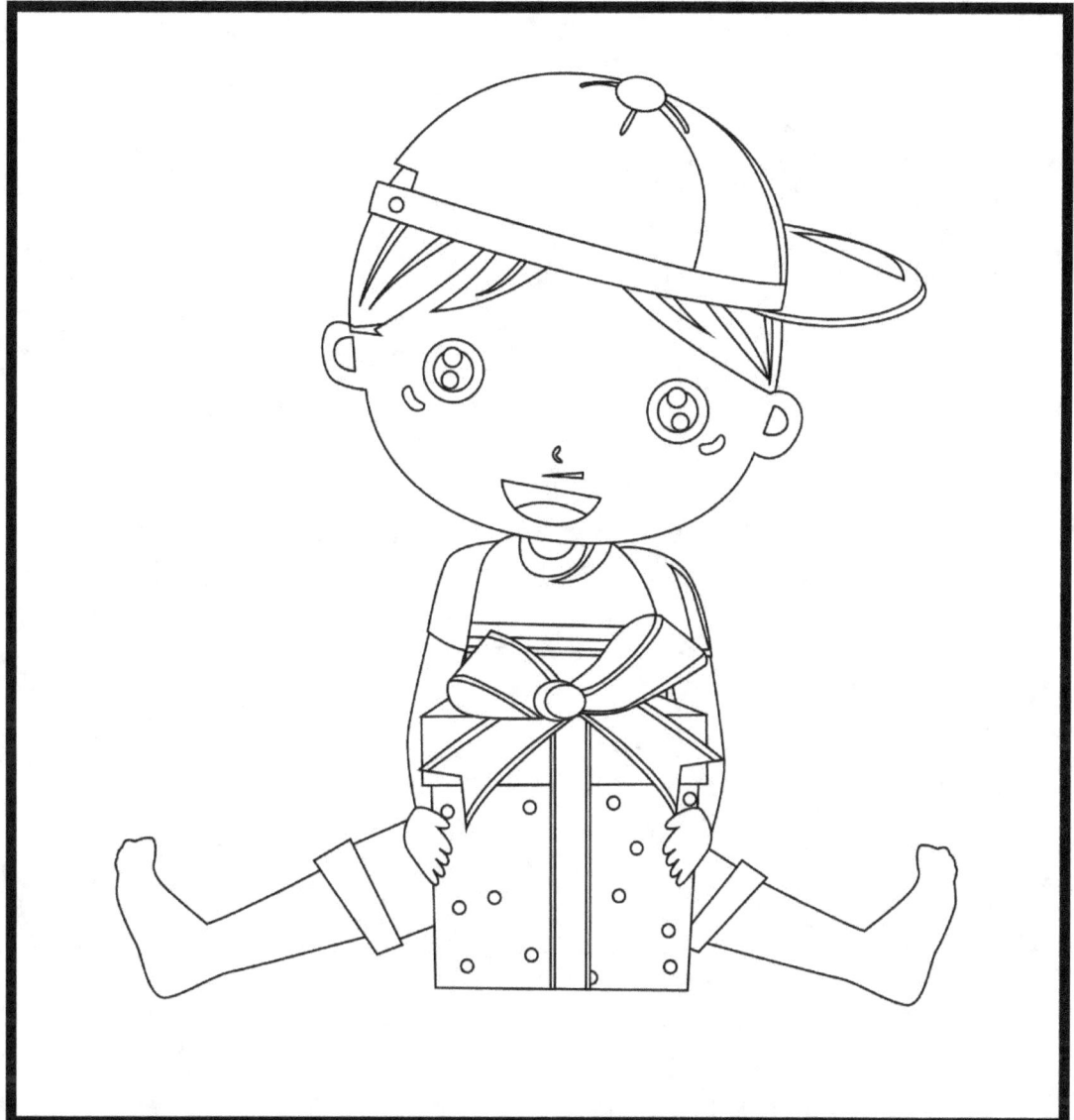

note:

_____

_____

_____

AUGUST 50TH

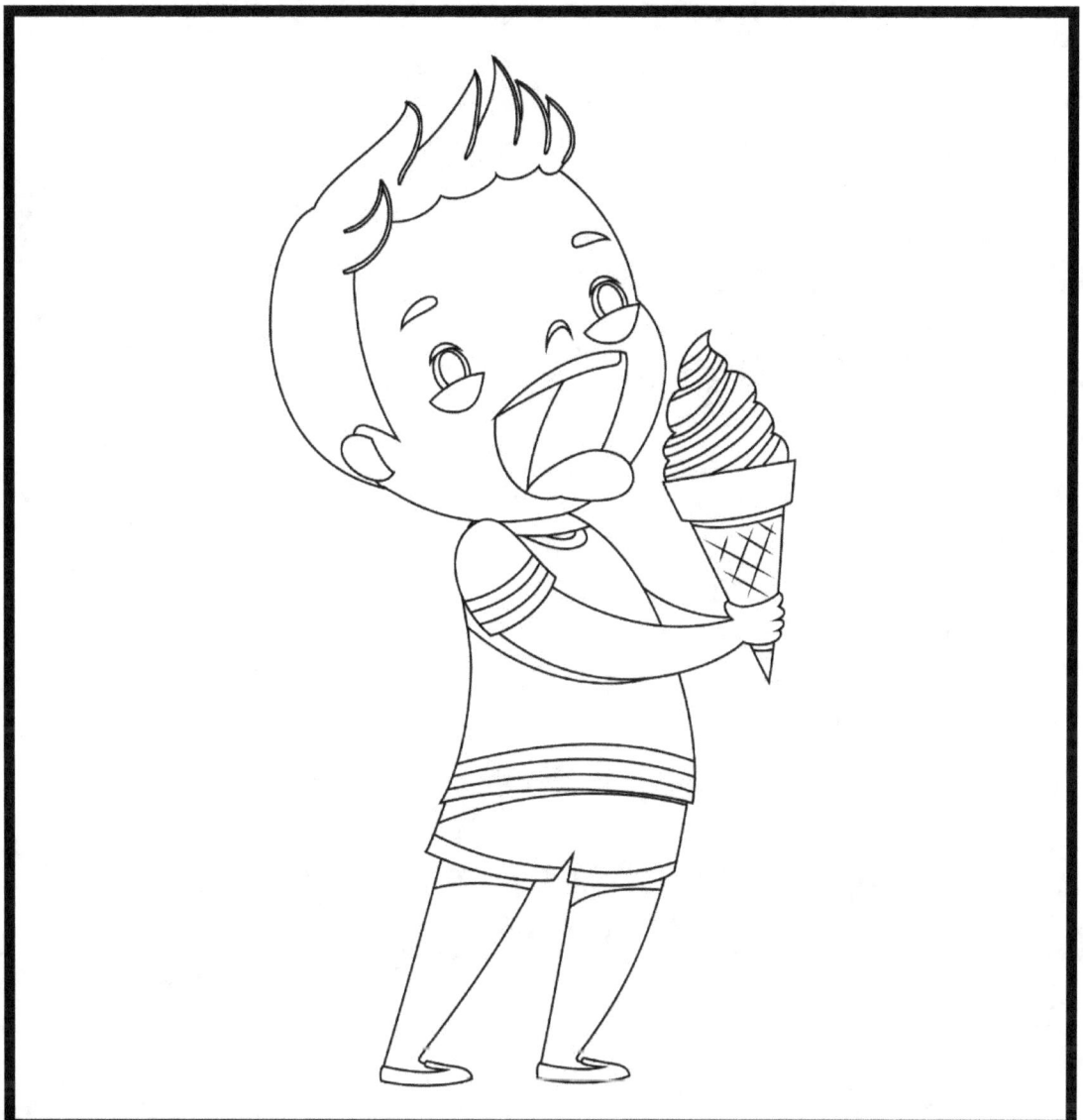

note:
_____

_____

_____